FISHES

OF THE SMOKIES

WRITTEN BY
GRANT FISHER

GREAT SMOKY MOUNTAINS
ASSOCIATION
Gatlinburg, Tennessee

EDITED BY: Aaron Searcy
SERIES DESIGN BY: Christina Watkins
BOOK DESIGN AND PRODUCTION BY: Lisa Horstman
EDITORIAL REVIEW AND ASSISTANCE BY: Frances Figart,
    Matt Kulp, and Rebecca Nichols
COVER PHOTO BY: Lance Merry
ILLUSTRATIONS BY: Cindy Day
PRINTED IN THE USA

1 2 3 4 5 6 7 8 9 10

ISBN 978-0-937207-02-4

Published by Great Smoky Mountains Association

Great Smoky Mountains Association is a nonprofit organization that supports the educational, scientific, and historical programs of Great Smoky Mountains National Park. Our publications are an educational service intended to enhance the public's understanding and enjoyment of the national park. If you would like to know more about our publications, memberships, and projects, please contact: Great Smoky Mountains Association, P.O. Box 130, Gatlinburg, TN, 37738 865.436.7318 SmokiesInformation.org

To my family and loved ones
for all their support and encouragement
throughout my life.

~Grant Fisher

CONTENTS

INTRODUCTION

 Just beneath the surface of most any larger stream in Great Smoky Mountains National Park is a world swimming with color. Flashes of blue, red, orange, silver, gold, tan, and even green can be seen darting about in the cool mountain waters on fishes of all shapes and sizes. Smokies streams are home to prehistoric fishes, iconic game fishes, culturally significant fishes, nocturnal fishes, native fishes, non-native fishes, jawless fishes, federally threatened and endangered fishes, as well as one species whose kin are mostly found in salt water. This guide is intended to enhance the reader's understanding of the many fish species that call the Smokies home.

The beautiful streams and rivers within Great Smoky Mountains National Park (GSMNP) include some of the richest fish species diversity in the United States. The park is home to approximately 80 species of fish represented by 12 different fish families including

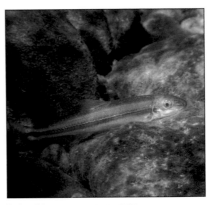

Fatlips Minnow. *Image by Derek Wheaton.*

sought-after game fish like trout and bass; colorful percids like the darters; the largest group, the minnows; the captivating suckers; and the obscure and mysterious lampreys, just to name a few. Many of these species are sensitive to environmental stressors and serve as important health indicators for the waterways they inhabit. Some fish species are very common and can be found throughout the lower-elevation streams in the park, while others are nocturnal and rarely seen. Three are classified as federally threatened or endangered species. Non-native fish species are also present in park waters, some of which are considered invasive and can displace native fishes.

SMOKIES STREAMS

GSMNP is known as a "headwaters park" as its borders encompass 41 major watersheds and include just over 2,900 miles of streams and rivers. These bodies of water range in size from the smallest first-order streams to large fifth-order rivers. Many of these streams consist of cold-water habitat, but others are cool-water streams with greater fish, habitat, and aquatic insect diversity.

Park watershed elevations range from 850 feet at the mouth of Abrams Creek to roughly 6,642 feet at Clingmans Dome. Mean stream gradients range from 1 to 20 percent and typically consist of cobble— small and large boulders with some bedrock outcroppings mixed in. Waterfalls and cascades are common and can act as upstream barriers to fish movement in some cases.

First-order streams account for about two-thirds of all GSMNP waterways, but the larger-order streams, orders two through five, are home to most of the fishes in the park. First-order headwater streams and smaller tributaries are usually too small for trout or other fish species to live in.

HOW GEOLOGICAL HISTORY AFFECTS FISHES

GSMNP lies within the Blue Ridge province, which is thought to have formed between 200 and 700 million years ago. Most park streams flow across sandstone, which overlays younger sedimentary rocks such as limestone. In some areas of the park and the surrounding region—such as in Cades Cove, Wears Cove, Tuckaleechee Cove, and West Miller Cove—the sandstone has been worn down, exposing a window of underlying limestone geology. Although sandstone is relatively insoluble, limestone is very soluble in water.

Most sandstone streams across the park are infertile with low mineral content, like distilled water. These are clear, cold, low-productivity streams with relatively poor acid buffering capacity. These streams produce a large diversity of aquatic insects but in low densities. Some high-elevation streams above 3,000 feet have an average stream pH of less than 6.0, which causes stress to Brook Trout and aquatic insects due to the acidity.

In contrast, streams underlain with limestone such as Abrams Creek and Hesse Creek support not only diverse but higher-density populations of aquatic insects and generally have higher fish-carrying capacities due to their greater productivity. In limestone watersheds, streams regularly "dry up" or go subterranean in summertime for large sections before re-emerging in a series of springs. These springs are home to some unique fishes like the Flame Chub (p. 75), which are rare in the park.

Fossil evidence in landscapes surrounding GSMNP suggests lower-elevation areas around the park were inundated by a shallow sea during the Paleozoic Era roughly 540 to 250 million years ago. As saltwater receded and was replaced by streams and rivers, some of the saltwater fishes, such as silversides, stayed behind. Although most silversides are found in saltwater, the Brook Silverside (p. 32) is found in medium-to-large rivers near the park boundary. Other possible saltwater leftovers include the Mountain Brook Lamprey and American Brook Lamprey (pp. 130, 131).

DISTINGUISHING FISHES FROM OTHER ANIMALS

What makes a fish a fish? Fishes are generally defined as a group of cold-blooded, finned, aquatic vertebrates that respire by passing oxygenated water over gills. Fossil records indicate fishes first appeared on Earth about 500 million years ago. They are generally divided into three broad taxonomic groups: 1) Agnatha, the jawless fishes; 2) Chondrichthyes, jawed fishes that have skeletons made of cartilage; and 3) Osteichthyes, jawed fishes that have skeletons made of bone.

Of these three groups, Agnatha is represented by approximately 120 species worldwide. Chondrichthyes is the next largest group with about 1,200 species worldwide. Finally, Osteichthyes comprises the largest group with roughly 28,000 species worldwide, making it very diverse and the largest group of vertebrates in existence today.

As a group, fishes have a number of interesting features. They have the senses of sight, smell, touch, and taste. They can also detect changes in water chemistry and can feel vibrations. Most fish can see color and can also see in very dim light. Generally, the more nocturnal or night-active fish are the greater the diameters of their eyes. Species such as catfish have

FISH ANATOMY

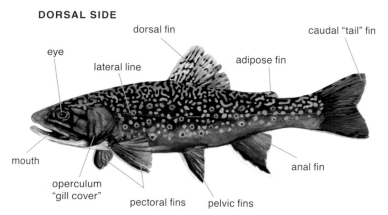

DORSAL SIDE

eye

dorsal fin

lateral line

caudal "tail" fin

adipose fin

mouth

operculum "gill cover"

pectoral fins

pelvic fins

anal fin

VENTRAL SIDE

a strong sense of smell and taste associated with their barbels and nostrils, which offsets the need for vision, and so their eye diameter is smaller.

All fishes have pairs of nostrils on each side of their heads that give them an excellent sense of taste and smell. Fishes such as trout can detect chemical levels as low as one part per billion. Like humans, fishes have taste buds on their tongues but also on their lips and mouths. Some also possess teeth on their tongues and some in their throats to help them catch, secure, and eat their prey.

Fishes have internal ear structures. Their ears use sets of small bones in gel-filled sacs called "otoliths" to maintain balance and help them hear underwater. Fishes also possess a lateral line to sense their surroundings. Pronounced in some species and unrecognizable in others, this line runs down the side of the body from the base of the tail to a location just behind the gills. The lateral line allows fishes to detect movements and vibrations around them and helps schooling fish to synchronize their movements.

Many species of fish also have scales that help protect their bodies. Fish that have small, soft scales tend to swim fast, and those that have large, hard scales tend to swim slower. The scales lay down daily growth rings (circuli) like on a tree and so can be used to determine a fish's age. These circuli grow closer together when daily growth slows, which usually delineates an annual mark (annuli). Otoliths, the inner ears of fishes, also have growth rings (circuli and annuli) like scales and can also be used by biologists to determine the age of fishes.

Most fishes produce slime, which has several important roles. Slime helps fishes maintain an ion balance in their bodies, provides external protection from parasites and wounds, and reduces drag when swimming.

Given they are a prey species, most fishes have darker colors on the top of their body and lighter colors on the bottom. This countershading allows them to blend into the substrate when overhead predators such as birds or mammals try to eat them and blend into the sky when benthic predators such as turtles, snakes or hellbenders try to eat them from below. Countershading is so effective that it is used by many other animals, birds, and even the military to blend in for similar reasons.

Fishes are unique in that they breathe, move waste products, and regulate ions in their bodies through their gills. They use their gills to gather oxygen from the water and release carbon dioxide from their bodies. However, fishes also move other waste like acids and ammonia out through their gills. Finally, some fishes have another adaptation called a swim bladder, an internal organ that can be filled with air to help the fish control its buoyancy. The swim bladder also helps the fish receive sound.

Fishes have a variety of fascinating adaptations that allow them to live in a wide range of freshwater habitats.

IDENTIFYING FISH SPECIES

What makes one fish different from another? In most cases, fish species are distinguished and identified using differences in body shape, numbers of fins, scales, fin rays, markings, colorations, the position of body parts such as the mouth, and the presence or absence of certain structures like barbels or adipose fins. In most cases, fishes can be identified using only external features. Because color and size can vary among individuals according to age, sex, and season, these are not always reliable ways to identify fish. The most precise tool to use to identify different fish species is a dichotomous key, as it lists numerous observable traits to distinguish one species from another. For this guide, we will use physical characteristics that make each species unique and will assist in identifying fishes in the field.

WHERE CAN I CATCH FISH?

Although there are roughly 2,900 miles of streams in the park, most of these streams are too small to support fish populations. NPS trout distribution surveys determined trout occupy only about 20 percent of these streams (580 miles). There are five species of game fish present in GSMNP, which include three trout and two bass species. These are the only fish species anglers can legally harvest within the park.

The Brook Trout (p. 148) is the only native trout species. It is found mostly in mid- to high-elevation streams above 3,000 feet and occupies about 43 percent of the park's 580 miles with trout. Although Brook Trout can grow to sizes of 10 to 15 inches, most only reach 7 to 8 inches as they are often found in small headwater streams that don't provide the food base to reach larger sizes.

Brown Trout (p. 147) are found mostly in lower-elevation sections of some large streams such as Little River, Oconaluftee River, Straight Fork, Cataloochee Creek, and most streams that flow into Fontana Reservoir. Once they reach a size of 8 inches, Brown Trout mostly eat other fish affording the protein needed to grow much larger, up to sizes of 25 to 30 inches. Brown Trout occupy about 23 percent of the 580 miles of trout streams.

Rainbow Trout (p. 146) are found in most streams across the park and are the most common trout species. They are mostly insectivores and rarely reach sizes greater than 12 to 14 inches in GSMNP streams. Rainbow Trout occupy about 76 percent of the 580 miles of trout streams.

Although Rainbow Trout spawn in the spring (March–April), Brook and Brown trout typically spawn in the fall (September–October for Brook; October–November for Brown). Readers should note that Rainbow Trout and Steelhead Trout are the same species; Steelhead are simply Rainbow Trout that migrate to and from the ocean to their native stream often several times in their lives.

Anglers can view what trout species are found in various park streams using the online trout distribution map available through the National Park Service website and the free ArcGIS map portal found there.

Two species of bass can be caught by anglers within the park: Rock Bass and Smallmouth Bass, both of which are found in the lower elevations of Abrams Creek, Little River, Middle and West Prongs of the Little Pigeon River, Oconaluftee River, and most large tributary streams to Fontana Reservoir. Rock Bass can reach sizes of 7 to 9 inches, while Smallmouth Bass can reach sizes close to 20 inches. Anglers should check the GSMNP fishing regulations on the National Park Service website for more info.

IS IT SAFE TO EAT BASS AND TROUT IN GSMNP?

The US Geological Survey, the Tennessee Department of Environment and Conservation, and the National Park Service conducted a multi-year, multi-park study that revealed certain fishes from federal lands contained levels of mercury exceeding human health standards. The nationwide study, conducted from 2008 to 2016, collected over 3,900 fish from 55 national parks, including 254 Brook, Brown, and Rainbow trout as well as Smallmouth Bass from 17 sites within GSMNP. Mercury levels from Brook, Brown, and Rainbow trout indicated they did not exceed human consumption advisory levels and therefore are safe to eat. However, nearly all the Smallmouth Bass greater than seven inches in length exceeded human health standards for mercury. With the exceptions of Brown Trout and Smallmouth Bass, other trout species generally do not live much longer than three years in park waters. The longer the fish lives, the greater amount of mercury it can absorb into its tissue.

Mercury is a toxic global contaminant that threatens resources the National Park Service is charged with protecting. Although there are natural sources of mercury such as volcanoes, it is estimated that as much as 75 percent of the mercury entering the atmosphere is from anthropogenic (human-caused) sources such as combustion; steel, iron, coke, and lime production; smelting; petroleum refining; and mercury cell chlor-alkali

Image by Bill Lea

production. Once in aquatic systems, biological (microbial) and chemical processes convert these forms into methylmercury, which can become concentrated in living organisms and move up the food chain. These pollutants are then taken up by soils, plants, animals, and fish. While a 10-to-13-inch Smallmouth Bass may not seem large to some anglers, a fish that size in GSMNP may be 8 to 10 years old, which is old enough to accumulate more contaminants in its tissue. Smallmouth Bass collected for this study began to show levels of mercury unsuitable for human consumption at a size of about seven inches.

If anglers do wish to eat Smallmouth, they should restrict consumption to no more than 1.2 pounds per month or one or two meals per month. Children, pregnant women, and nursing mothers should avoid eating any amount of these fish. For more information on the Smallmouth Bass Mercury Consumption Advisory, please see the GSMNP Smallmouth Bass webpage.

FISH STOCKING

By the time GSMNP was established in 1934, visitor experiences such as fishing were such a priority that local anglers had stocked non-native Rainbow Trout into nearly every major watershed in the park. Early park managers also believed that trout stocking was necessary to provide a good angling experience, so they readily stocked Rainbow Trout and a northern hatchery strain of Brook Trout across park steams. In addition, Civilian Conservation Corp crews built NPS-operated trout hatcheries at Kephart Prong and Chimneys picnic area to help supplement trout being stocked from other area hatcheries. Between 1934 and 1975, more than 800,000 hatchery-strain Brook Trout and 1.4 million Rainbow Trout were stocked across GSMNP streams.

In the 1970s, park managers noticed that, in many of the streams where Rainbow Trout were stocked, they had displaced or extirpated the native Brook Trout. As national parks are generally set aside to protect and preserve native species, park managers realized stocking non-native fish did not match up with their own park policies. Therefore, trout stocking operations in GSMNP ceased in 1976.

Today, although not all trout caught in the park are native, most are considered wild and likely born within the park. Anglers in the park occasionally catch trout that have migrated into park streams after being stocked outside the park by the North Carolina Wildlife Resources Commission, the Tennessee Wildlife Resources Agency, or the Eastern Band of Cherokee Indians. These trout often have clipped or deformed fins indicative of spending time in a concrete raceway and are usually distinguishable from wild trout.

FISH PARASITES

Although the majority of the park's streams are clear and cold much of the year, most fishes that live in the park, like those in most other area waters, must contend with fish parasites. GSMNP studies indicate 66 percent of fish have at least one internal or external parasite, and some have as many as seven different types.

Most of these parasites are considered "commensal," meaning they do not harm the fish. Examples of parasites include leeches, roundworms, flukes, protozoans, flatworms, and even freshwater mussel larvae called Glochidia. Glochidia attach to the gills, fins, and bodies of host fish where they live and feed for a period of time before falling off to begin their adult lives buried in the gravel.

None of the parasites found in GSMNP fishes are the kind that would cause great harm to a species, and none of them would be harmful to a human if the fish to be consumed was properly cooked. Although finding such a variety of parasites sounds alarming, parasites are very common in most animals, including fishes. Parasites are just another example of the biodiversity found within GSMNP.

THREATS TO GSMNP FISH POPULATIONS

Although the waters of GSMNP appear to be clear, cold, and relatively unimpaired, there are some serious threats that affect Smokies fish populations. The greatest threat is the acidification of high-elevation soils and streams due to acid deposition or acid rain. Currently there are

12 GSMNP streams listed by the Environmental Protection Agency as "impaired" because they have a mean stream pH less than 6.0. These and other streams across GSMNP have received decades of pollutants such as nitrous oxides, sulfur dioxides, and ammonium through acid rain that has caused these streams to become acidified. Low stream pH can reduce fish and aquatic insect diversity, limit reproduction, and even kill fishes.

Other threats include fish diseases such as whirling disease, which affects trout and can lead to death. Another similar invasive threat is gill lice, which are tiny copepods that attach to the gills of trout and can kill them. Both whirling disease and gill lice are spread by moving infected fish from one water body to another. New Zealand mudsnails, didymo, and zebra and quagga mussels are all invasive and can harm native fish populations if they become established in local streams. These aquatic invasives are typically spread by clinging onto wading boots or waders, via boat hulls and bilges, or from dumping water from one infected water body into another.

Given these threats, it is important to clean and dry wading and snorkeling gear between streams to minimize the risk of spreading harmful invasives. Also, fish should never be caught in one stream and dumped into another. Anglers, snorkelers, kayakers, canoers, and anyone who likes to recreate in water should be aware of these threats and not be part of the problem.

One other serious threat to many fish species is the moving of rocks and creating of rock dams and cairns in streams, which has been made popular by social media images. Many fish species, including some of the federally threatened and endangered fishes, live and nest under dinner-plate-sized rocks. These species spawn in summer months when people tend to swim in streams. When a nest rock is disturbed, the male fish that guards the nest abandons the nest, making it vulnerable to fungus, predation, and death. Visitors should refrain from moving rocks and keep the native habitat in place in order to protect the Smokies' native species.

FEDERALLY THREATENED AND ENDANGERED FISH SPECIES

In 1957, the US Fish and Wildlife Service in cooperation with several state and federal agencies used the fish pesticide rotenone to remove

46 fish species, including four species now federally listed, from lower Abrams Creek. The purpose was to establish a trophy Rainbow Trout fishery in the newly built Chilhowee Reservoir. Application of the pesticide removed all native fish from the main stem of lower Abrams Creek downstream of Abrams Falls, formerly the most diverse stream in GSMNP.

Although roughly 35 of the 46 species recolonized lower Abrams Creek from other tributaries, roughly 10 species did not. The creation of Chilhowee Reservoir forever changed the lower sections of the stream into a reservoir embayment and effectively isolated Abrams Creek from recolonization by many naturally occurring species including Spotfin Chubs, Citico Darters (p. 115), and Smoky and Yellowfin madtom (pp. 102 and 103).

After the treatment, Smoky Madtom were presumed to be extinct until a 1980 discovery of a population in nearby Citico Creek in Monroe County, Tennessee. The Citico Creek population is still the only known naturally occurring population for Smoky Madtom. The Smoky Madtom was added to the endangered species list, under the Endangered Species Act, in October 1984. The Yellowfin Madtom was added to the threatened list in 1977.

Since the mid-1980s, NPS fisheries scientists have partnered with the nonprofit organization Conservation Fisheries to rear and restore the four threatened and endangered species of fish that were historically found here. Restoration efforts for the federally endangered Smoky Madtom and Citico Darter, along with the federally threatened Yellowfin Madtom, have had great success, and each of these three species is now naturally reproducing in Abrams Creek. Unfortunately, efforts to restore Spotfin Chub populations have had no success, likely due to the absence of a large riverine system downstream of Abrams Creek where they were stocked. That portion of the Little Tennessee River is now part of Chilhowee Reservoir.

NATIVE FISH RESTORATION

State and federal agencies have also worked to reintroduce several other species that have not naturally recolonized. These include campaigns to reintroduce the Greenside Darter and Banded Sculpin from source populations in lower Little River just outside the park. Restoring these species would not only help reestablish the native fish fauna of Abrams Creek but also provide additional host fish that native mussels need to reproduce and help set the stage for reintroducing other native mussels that were likely extirpated during the 1957 rotenone treatment.

The Brook Trout is another fish species that has been the focus of restoration efforts in certain GSMNP streams. Brook Trout (*Salvelinus fontinalis*) are the only trout species native to the Smokies and Appalachian Mountains. Historically, they were found in most park streams, but in the early 1900s, logging operations greatly reduced their populations and destroyed much of their habitat. Readily available Rainbow Trout were introduced into many park streams to provide recreational fishing opportunities, but they were able to produce twice the number of eggs, grow faster, and out compete native Brook Trout where the two species mixed. By 1934, Brook Trout lost more of their range, and Rainbow Trout were established in nearly every park watershed. The NPS continued to raise and stock over 1.4 million Rainbow Trout across park streams until 1975 when they realized they were threatening native Brook Trout populations.

SNORKELING TO SEE GSMNP FISHES

Freshwater snorkeling is an enjoyable way to see the often otherwise invisible aquatic world. The larger, low-elevation streams of the Smokies have clear water and a diverse array of aquatic life, which creates the perfect combination for snorkeling. The clear water allows for easy observation and photographing of many colorful fishes, crayfishes, turtles, aquatic macroinvertebrates, and salamanders. Snorkeling also affords an opportunity to view fish and their natural behaviors in their preferred habitats as they forage for food, spar for territory, and even construct their nests.

The only materials needed to get started are a mask, snorkel, and some closed-toed shoes. An old pair of tennis shoes works great. Masks and snorkels come in a few different styles. The traditional two-piece style of mask and snorkel can be purchased for less than $30 and works extremely well.

Because the waters of the park are cold, many people prefer to wear a 5mm or 7mm wetsuit, but any wetsuit will help maintain body temperature. A towel, change of clothes, sunscreen, and a water bottle can be helpful when snorkeling. Some snorkelers enjoy underwater photography, which requires a waterproof camera or a waterproof housing for non-waterproof cameras.

Choosing the proper location is one of the keys for ensuring a safe and enjoyable snorkeling trip. Factors to consider are habitat, water temperature, depth, clarity, and waterbody size. A good place to start is on a satellite map with a street-view application. Here in the park, lower-gradient streams and streams below 2,000 feet in elevation are good places to see a diverse range of aquatic organisms.

~ Matt Kulp, NPS supervisory fisheries biologist

Fisheries Work in the Smokies

Great Smoky Mountains National Park fisheries biologists are responsible for collecting important data about fishes in the Smokies, sampling and analyzing waterway quality, managing sustainable game fish populations, and restoring and monitoring multiple threatened and endangered species within the park.

Like other aquatic creatures, fishes are sensitive organisms that are significantly impacted by changes in water quality or stream structure. Fisheries staff conduct routine *E. coli* sampling in high-use areas to monitor bacterial levels in certain streams and propose solutions. Acid deposition surveys are also conducted by park staff as well as volunteers, and water samples are collected and sent to a laboratory for in-depth chemical analysis.

To monitor fish populations, fisheries biologists conduct multifaceted studies each year to keep track of changes and gain a better understanding of developing trends. Yearly monitoring functions as a way to check up on different stream populations.

Fisheries workers typically operate in teams and use a method of sampling known as "three-pass depletion." Equipped with a backpack shocker, one person stuns fishes and passes them to a netter, who then passes the fishes to someone carrying a bucket. Fisheries employees make three passes through the site in total. After each pass, fishes are identified, counted, weighed, and measured.

While many of the streams in the Smokies are sampled using three-pass depletion methodology, some are simply too large and require a different type of sampling. The index of biotic integrity, or IBI, is used on larger park streams that would be difficult to sample successfully using three-pass depletion due to the large crew numbers required. When conducting an IBI sample, fisheries staff use a large mesh seine to sample riffle, run, and pool areas. Fishes are found in a variety of habitats, and the IBI method of sampling aims to collect fishes out of all available habitats in order to find out the population abundance. It is through this type of sampling that many nongame fish species such as darters are collected.

In order to monitor the populations of threatened and endangered fish, park scientists conduct yearly snorkel surveys. This collection of yearly

Workers use backpack electrofishing units to stun fish for netting and capturing the non-native Rainbow Trout. *NPS photo.*

data is extremely important in determining if the restocked populations of fish are indeed thriving.

Much of the data about fishes in the Smokies, including fundamental information presented in this guide, would not exist without years of hard work by fisheries staff.

Fish Checklist

☐ Brook Silverside
Labidesthes sicculus
☐ White Sucker
Catostomus commersonii
☐ Northern Hogsucker
Hypentelium nigricans
☐ River Redhorse
Moxostoma carinatum
☐ Black Redhorse
Moxostoma duquesnei
☐ Golden Redhorse
Moxostoma erythrurum
☐ Sicklefin Redhorse
Moxostoma sp.
☐ Smallmouth Redhorse
Moxostoma breviceps
☐ Rock Bass *Ambloplites rupestris*
☐ Redbreast Sunfish
Lepomis auritus
☐ Green Sunfish
Lepomis cyanellus
☐ Warmouth *Lepomis gulosus*
☐ Bluegill *Lepomis macrochirus*
☐ Longear Sunfish
Lepomis megalotis
☐ Redear Sunfish
Lepomis microlophus
☐ Largemouth Bass
Micropterus salmoides
☐ Spotted Bass
Micropterus punctulatus
☐ Smallmouth Bass
Micropterus dolomieu

☐ White Crappie
Pomoxis annularis
☐ Black Crappie
Pomoxis nigromaculatus
☐ White Bass *Morone chrysops*
☐ Gizzard Shad
Dorosoma cepedianum
☐ Mottled Sculpin *Cottus bairdii*
☐ Banded Sculpin *Cottus carolinae*
☐ Central Stoneroller
Campostoma anomalum
☐ Rosyside Dace
Clinostomus funduloides
☐ Whitetail Shiner
Cyprinella galactura
☐ Flame Chub *Hemitremia flammea*
☐ Bigeye Chub *Hybopsis amblops*
☐ Striped Shiner
Luxilus chrysocephalus
☐ Warpaint Shiner
Luxilus coccogenis
☐ River Chub *Nocomis micropogon*
☐ Tennessee Shiner
Notropis leuciodus
☐ Silver Shiner *Notropis photogenis*
☐ Saffron Shiner
Notropis rubricroceus
☐ Emerald Shiner
Notropis atherinoides
☐ Mirror Shiner
Notropis spectrunculus
☐ Telescope Shiner
Notropis telescopus

☐ Fatlips Minnow
Phenacobius crassilabrum
☐ Tennessee Dace
Chrosomus tennesseensis
☐ Fathead Minnow
Pimephales promelas
☐ Eastern Blacknose Dace
Rhinichthys atratulus
☐ Longnose Dace
Rhinichthys cataractae
☐ Creek Chub
Semotilus atromaculatus
☐ Common Carp
Cyprinus carpio
☐ Goldfish *Carassius auratus*
☐ Longnose Gar *Lepisosteus osseus*
☐ Yellow Bullhead
Ameiurus natalis
☐ Black Bullhead *Ameiurus melas*
☐ Smoky Madtom *Noturus baileyi*
☐ Yellowfin Madtom
Noturus flavipinnis
☐ Flathead Catfish
Pylodictis olivaris
 Blue Catfish *Ictalurus furcatus*
☐ Channel Catfish
Ictalurus punctatus
☐ Greenside Darter
Etheostoma blennioides
☐ Greenfin Darter
Etheostoma chlorobranchium
☐ Fantail Darter
Etheostoma flabellare
☐ Tuckasegee Darter
Etheostoma gutselli

☐ Blueside Darter
Etheostoma jessiae
☐ Citico Darter
Etheostoma sitikuense
☐ Redline Darter
Etheostoma rufilineatum
☐ Tennessee Snubnose Darter
Etheostoma simoterum
☐ Swannanoa Darter
Etheostoma swannanoa
☐ Wounded Darter
Etheostoma vulneratum
☐ Banded Darter *Etheostoma zonale*
☐ Yellow Perch *Perca flavescens*
☐ Tangerine Darter
Percina aurantiaca
☐ Logperch *Percina caprodes*
☐ Gilt Darter *Percina evides*
☐ Olive Darter *Percina squamata*
☐ Walleye *Sander vitreus*
☐ Sauger *Sander canadense*
☐ Mountain Brook Lamprey
Ichthyomyzon greeleyi
☐ American Brook Lamprey
Lethenteron appendix
☐ Western Mosquitofish
Gambusia affinis
☐ Northern Studfish
Fundulus catenatus
☐ Freshwater Drum
Aplodinotus grunniens
☐ Rainbow Trout
Oncorhynchus mykiss
☐ Brown Trout *Salmo trutta*
☐ Brook Trout *Salvelinus fontinalis*

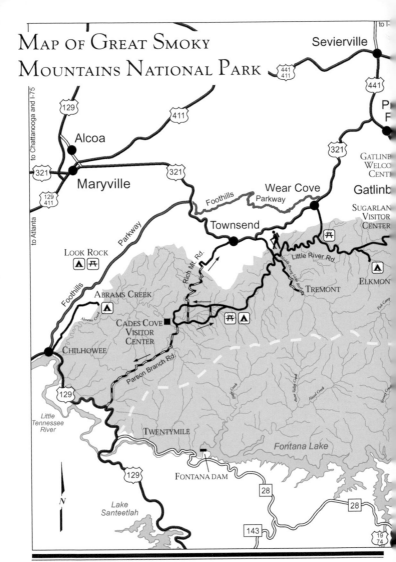

MAP OF GREAT SMOKY
MOUNTAINS NATIONAL PARK

Sevierville

Alcoa

Maryville

Wear Cove

Foothills Parkway

Townsend

Gatlinb

GATLINB
WELCO
CENT

Gatlinb

SUGARLAN
VISITOR
CENTER

LOOK ROCK

Rich Mt. Rd.

Little River Rd.

TREMONT

ELKMON

ABRAMS CREEK

CADES COVE
VISITOR
CENTER

CHILHOWEE

Parson Branch Rd.

Little
Tennessee
River

TWENTYMILE

Fontana Lake

FONTANA DAM

Lake
Santeetlah

N

to Chattanooga and I-75

to Atlanta

Foothills

Parkway

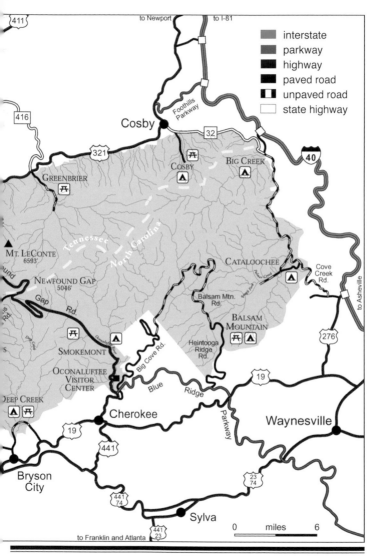

interstate
parkway
highway
paved road
unpaved road
state highway

to Newport
to I-81
411
416
Cosby
Foothills Parkway
32
321
COSBY
BIG CREEK
40
GREENBRIER
Tennessee
North Carolina
MT. LECONTE
6593'
CATALOOCHEE
Cove Creek Rd.
NEWFOUND GAP
5046'
Gap Rd.
Balsam Mtn. Rd.
to Asheville
BALSAM MOUNTAIN
276
SMOKEMONT
Heintooga Ridge Rd.
OCONALUFTEE VISITOR CENTER
Big Cove Rd.
Blue
Ridge
19
DEEP CREEK
Cherokee
Waynesville
19
Parkway
441
Bryson City
23
74
441
74
Sylva
441
23
to Franklin and Atlanta
0   miles   6

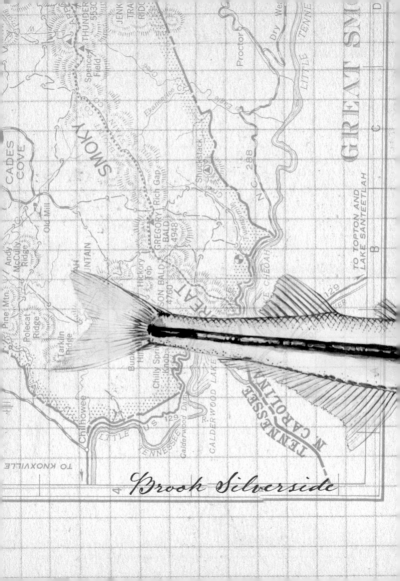

Brook Silverside

Neotropical Silversides

Family Atherinopsidae

Brook Silverside

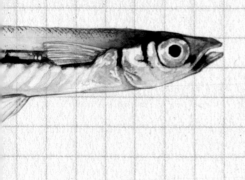

BROOK SILVERSIDE

Image by Adam Walker

Labidesthes sicculus

Size: Up to 5 in (13 cm)

GREAT SMOKY MOUNTAINS
NATIONAL PARK

◆ **Description:** The Brook Silverside is a slender, thin fish with a pointed mouth and silver-colored lateral stripe. Reaching a maximum size of five inches, they serve as an important food source for predatory lake fish such as bass and Walleye. Silversides primarily feed on zooplankton and rarely live more than a year. They are often observed schooling near the surface, where some may jump if a predatory fish is nearby.

◆ **Habitat:** Known to live in lakes, reservoirs, and large rivers. They are not found in smaller streams.

◆ **Range:** Mississippi River drainage south to Louisiana, Florida, and other areas in eastern North America. In the Smokies, they are only found in the embayed section of Abrams Creek on Chilhowee Reservoir.

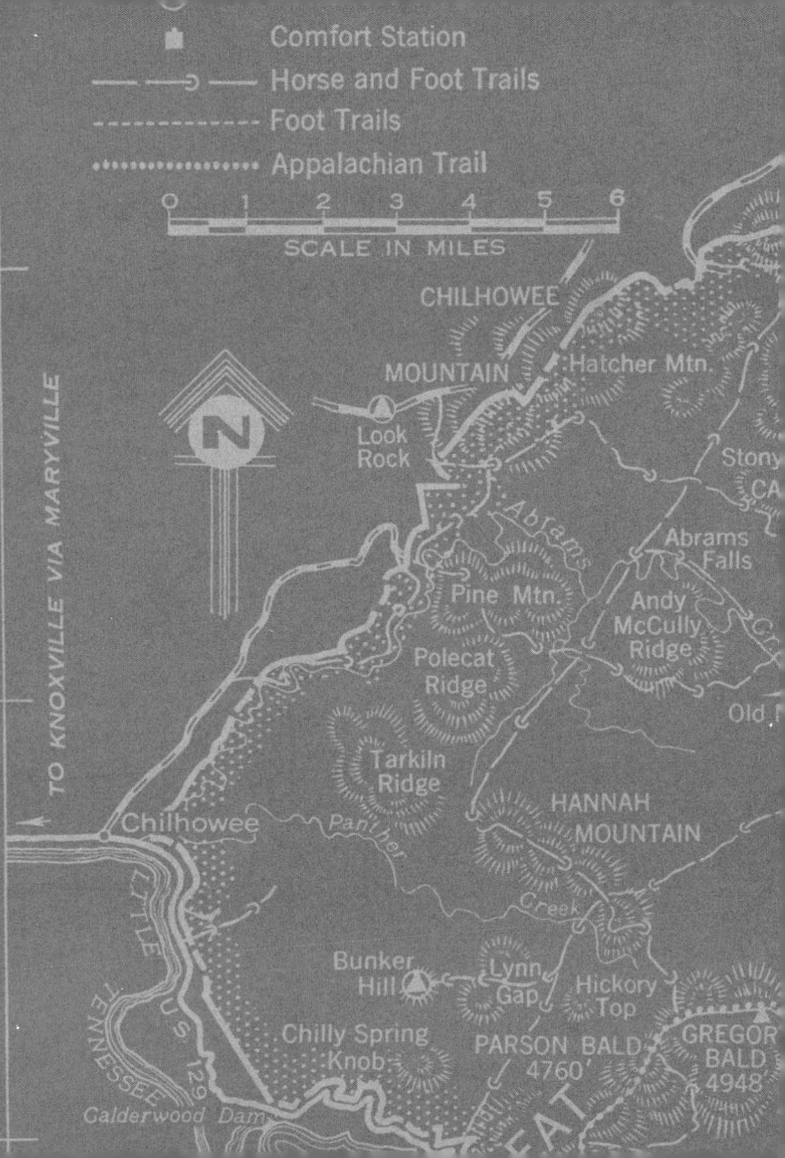

Legend

■ Comfort Station

——— ——o—— Horse and Foot Trails

- - - - - - - - - Foot Trails

•••••••••••••• Appalachian Trail

SCALE IN MILES
0 1 2 3 4 5 6

N

CHILHOWEE

MOUNTAIN   Hatcher Mtn.

Look
Rock

Abrams

Stony

CA

Abrams
Falls

Pine Mtn.

Andy
McCully
Ridge

Polecat
Ridge

Old

TO KNOXVILLE VIA MARYVILLE

Tarkiln
Ridge

Panther

HANNAH

MOUNTAIN

Chilhowee

Creek

LITTLE
TENNESSEE
US 129

Bunker
Hill

Lynn
Gap

Hickory
Top

Chilly Spring
Knob

PARSON BALD
4760'

GREGOR
BALD
4948'

Calderwood Dam

EAT

Sichlefin Redhorse

SUCKERS

Family Catostomidae

White Sucker

Northern Hogsucker

River Redhorse

Black Redhorse

Golden Redhorse

Sicklefin Redhorse

Smallmouth Redhorse

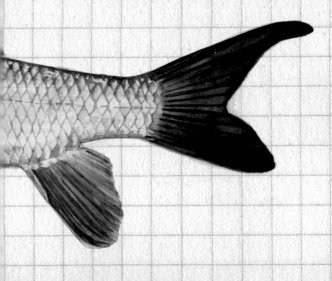

WHITE SUCKER

Image by Adam Walker

Catostomus commersonii
Size: 6–9 in (15–23 cm)

GREAT SMOKY MOUNTAINS
NATIONAL PARK

◆ **Description:** White Suckers resemble red-horse suckers but have more lateral line scales (60–70). Sizes of six to nine inches are common, but they can grow to nearly two feet and live 17 years. As with many fish species, juveniles feed on plankton, while adults primarily eat benthic macroinvertebrates. White Suckers were a major food source for the Cherokee as well as other Native American tribes. Large rock weirs were constructed to trap migrating suckers for collection. Many of these weirs can still be found to this day during periods of low water flow.

◆ **Habitat:** Often found in pool areas of spring-fed streams but also occurs in cool lakes.

◆ **Range:** Found throughout much of eastern North America, the Midwest, and north into Canada. In the Smokies, they are found in Abrams Creek and rarely occur in Little River, Cataloochee Creek, Oconaluftee River, Deep Creek, and Twentymile Creek.

Image courtesy of ncfishes.com

◆ **Description:** The Northern Hogsucker has a very distinctive appearance. It has a characteristic "sucker" mouth, which is specially adapted for feeding on aquatic insect larvae and snails. Minnow species commonly follow feeding hogsuckers as they stir up debris and potential food items. Fish in the six-to-nine-inch range are common, but they can reach two feet in reservoir areas.

◆ **Habitat:** Occurs in all stream habitats but prefers riffle areas.

◆ **Range:** Wide ranging. Found in the Mississippi River drainage, east to the Atlantic coast. Population range extends south to northern Georgia and Alabama. They are found in all stream systems in GSMNP up to 3,000 feet.

Hypentelium nigricans
Size: 6–9 in (15–23 cm)

GREAT SMOKY MOUNTAINS
NATIONAL PARK

RIVER REDHORSE

Image by Bernard Kuhajda

Moxostoma carinatum

Size: Up to 3 ft (91 cm)

GREAT SMOKY MOUNTAINS
NATIONAL PARK

◆ **Description:** River Redhorse are most easily identified by their distinctive red caudal fin and number of lateral line scales (42-44). Occasionally taken on rod and reel, they are known to put up quite a fight. Adult River Redhorse feed on freshwater bivalves such as mussels and the introduced Asian clam.

◆ **Habitat:** Swift waters of larger rivers. They enter smaller streams during spawning.

◆ **Range:** Occurs in the Mississippi River drainage. While uncommon in the Smokies, they are found in the embayed section of Abrams Creek and other streams draining into the Little Tennessee River. Much of its range has been reduced due to the construction of hydroelectric dams.

BLACK REDHORSE

Image by Bryson Hilburn

◆ **Description:** The Black Redhorse differs
from other redhorse species by having 44 to
48 lateral line scales. It is nearly identical to
the Golden Redhorse and can grow to nearly
two feet. They feed primarily on small crustaceans and midge larvae. Black Redhorse are
the most common redhorse sucker found in
GSMNP.
◆ **Habitat:** Prefers clear, cool creeks and small
rivers. Occasionally found in lakes.
◆ **Range:** Occurs in the Mississippi River
drainage. It is found in all major park streams
except those in the Pigeon River drainage.
Black Redhorse are widespread across much
of Tennessee.

*Moxostoma
duquesnei*
Size: Up to 2 ft (61 cm)

GREAT SMOKY MOUNTAINS
NATIONAL PARK

GOLDEN REDHORSE

Image by Bernard Kuhajda

*Moxostoma
erythrurum*

Size: Up to 3 ft (91 cm)

GREAT SMOKY MOUNTAINS
NATIONAL PARK

◆ **Description:** Very similar in appearance to the Black Redhorse and often found in the same areas. Golden Redhorse can be identified by their 39 to 43 lateral line scales. Bottom fins are usually orange, while dorsal and caudal fins are gray. Like other redhorse suckers, they undergo a spring spawning run into smaller bodies of water. Food items include small bivalves along with midge and caddisfly larvae.

◆ **Habitat:** Golden Redhorse are more tolerant of larger water than Black Redhorse are. They are typically found in large creeks and smaller rivers where they prefer deep, slow-moving water.

◆ **Range:** Mississippi River drainage north to the Great Lakes region. Found in several Little Tennessee River drainage systems in the park, from the Oconaluftee River to Abrams Creek. Rare in the Little Pigeon River.

SICKLEFIN REDHORSE

Image by Luke Etchison

◆ **Description:** While the Sicklefin Redhorse is uncommon, it is a very recognizable fish. Adults are identified by their distinctive tall "sickle-shaped" dorsal fin. They primarily feed on aquatic insects and aquatic vegetation. A great amount of work has been done towards the conservation and restoration of the Sicklefin Redhorse. Historically, they inhabited most streams in the Blue Ridge region, but populations have been greatly reduced due to excess runoff, pollution, and construction of hydroelectric dams. Due to the need for clean, clear water, their populations are still at risk from anthropogenic influences.

◆ **Habitat:** Reservoirs and streams of moderate-to-fast flow.

◆ **Range:** Hiawassee and Little Tennessee River systems. In the Smokies, they are rare but can be found in lower Noland Creek, Forney Creek, and the Oconaluftee and Tuckasegee Rivers just outside the park boundary.

Moxostoma sp.

Size: Up to 2 ft (61 cm)

GREAT SMOKY MOUNTAINS NATIONAL PARK

SMALLMOUTH REDHORSE

Image by Noah Daun

Moxostoma breviceps

Size: Up to 20 in (51 cm)

GREAT SMOKY MOUNTAINS
NATIONAL PARK

◆ **Description:** The Smallmouth Redhorse is similar in appearance to other redhorse species, but it has a significantly smaller head and mouth. Smallmouth Redhorse have 41 to 45 lateral line scales and feed mostly on benthic macroinvertebrates.

◆ **Habitat:** Large fast-flowing rivers and reservoirs.

◆ **Range:** Found throughout the Ohio River drainage including the Tennessee and Cumberland river systems. They are extremely rare in the Smokies. Smallmouth Redhorse were last documented in the Little Tennessee River system in the 1980s.

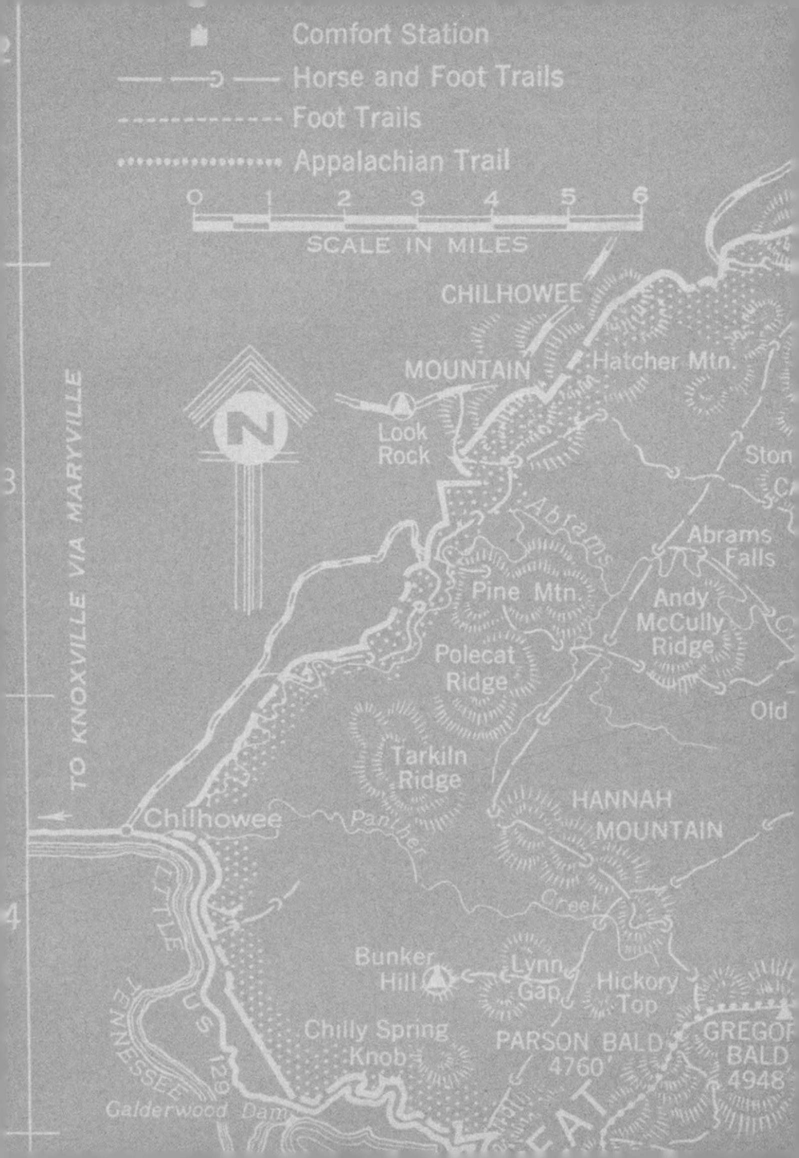

Legend

- 🏠 Comfort Station
- ——o—— Horse and Foot Trails
- ------------ Foot Trails
- •••••••••••••• Appalachian Trail

SCALE IN MILES
0 1 2 3 4 5 6

CHILHOWEE

MOUNTAIN — Hatcher Mtn.

Look Rock

Ston

Abrams

Abrams Falls

Pine Mtn.

Andy McCully Ridge

Polecat Ridge

Old

Tarkiln Ridge

Panther

HANNAH MOUNTAIN

Chilhowee

Creek

TO KNOXVILLE VIA MARYVILLE

Bunker Hill

Lynn Gap

Hickory Top

Chilly Spring Knob

PARSON BALD 4760'

GREGORY BALD 4948'

LITTLE TENNESSEE US 129

Calderwood Dam

GREAT

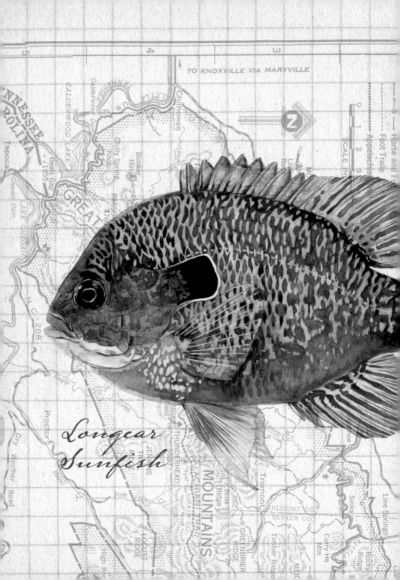

Longear
Sunfish

SUNFISH AND BASS
Family Centrarchidae

Rock Bass

Redbreast Sunfish

Green Sunfish

Warmouth

Bluegill

Longear Sunfish

Redear Sunfish

Largemouth Bass

Spotted Bass

Smallmouth Bass

White Crappie

Black Crappie

ROCK BASS

Image by Grant Fisher

Ambloplites
rupestris
Size: Up to 1 lb (½ kg)

GREAT SMOKY MOUNTAINS
NATIONAL PARK

◆ **Description:** Also known as "Redeye Bass," Rock Bass are easily distinguished by their characteristic red eyes and five to seven anal fin spines. They are commonly caught by trout and bass anglers on spinners, flies, and crankbaits when casting along stream banks. They can live up to eight years and typically weigh less than one pound.

◆ **Habitat:** Prefer sheltered pool areas, where they are often found under cover of root wads or dense brush.

◆ **Range:** Mississippi River drainage to Great Lakes and east to Atlantic coast. Common in all larger Smokies streams below 2,100 feet, except for those in the Pigeon River drainage.

REDBREAST SUNFISH

Image by Jason Lins

◆ **Description:** Redbreast Sunfish have a rounded body and are distinguished by their orange or red coloration during spawning season. The dorsal area is usually blue green in coloration, and they typically have horizontal blue stripes underneath their eyes. The Redbreast Sunfish diet consists of terrestrial insects, adult and larval aquatic insects, crustaceans, and even smaller fish.

◆ **Habitat:** More common in reservoir areas but can also be found in small creeks and rivers.

◆ **Range:** Native in Atlantic Coast drainages. Introduced to GSMNP and only rarely found in impounded areas of the Little Tennessee River. They are also found in the Little Pigeon River and Little River just beyond the park boundary.

Lepomis auritus
Size: Up to 10 in (25 cm)

GREAT SMOKY MOUNTAINS
NATIONAL PARK

GREEN SUNFISH

Image by Jason Lins

Lepomis cyanellus
Size: 5–8 in (13–20 cm)

GREAT SMOKY MOUNTAINS
NATIONAL PARK

◆ **Description:** Green Sunfish can be identified by their oval body shape and yellow pelvic fin coloration. The anal, caudal, and dorsal fins can also have yellow tips. These fish have a very large mouth compared to other sunfish. Green Sunfish tend to be very aggressive and defensive of nesting areas, and they will consume any available prey.

◆ **Habitat:** Very diverse habitat preferences. Green Sunfish can be found in ponds, lakes, large rivers, and small streams.

◆ **Range:** Widespread across the United States. Only collected in Hazel Creek and Eagle Creek in the Smokies but likely in all embayed areas of the Little Tennessee River.

WARMOUTH

Image by Grant Fisher

◆ **Description:** Warmouth resemble Rock
Bass in body shape but have a unique cam-
ouflage pattern with hints of black vertical
striping. They also have very dark eyes that
develop an opaque sheen. Three to four anal
fin spines are also present. While many sunfish nest in clean, shallow water, Warmouth
prefer more turbid, silty areas. They are
primarily bottom-feeding fish and prey upon
aquatic insects and crustaceans, such as
amphipods.

◆ **Habitat:** Lowland streams or lakes with
areas of dense cover.

◆ **Range:** Widespread across eastern North
America and the Mississippi River drainage.
Uncommon in the Smokies but can be found
in the reservoirs of the Little Tennessee River.

Lepomis gulosus
Size: 9 in (23 cm)

GREAT SMOKY MOUNTAINS
NATIONAL PARK

BLUEGILL

Image by Jason Lins

Lepomis macrochirus
Size: ½ lb (¼ kg)

GREAT SMOKY MOUNTAINS
NATIONAL PARK

♦ **Description:** Bluegill have a very circular body shape. Adults have eight to ten sets of doubled vertical bars and can have a yellow-orange belly. Like other sunfish, Bluegill create round gravel nests in slow-moving sections of streams or shallow lakes. Most stream Bluegill rarely exceed half a pound, while reservoir fish grow larger.

♦ **Habitat:** Inhabits lakes and streams. Prefers cover made by vegetation or submerged wood and rock.

♦ **Range:** Widespread across entire United States. In the park, Bluegill are found in the Little Tennessee River system from the Oconaluftee River to Abrams Creek. They are also found in the Little River and Little Pigeon River outside the park boundary.

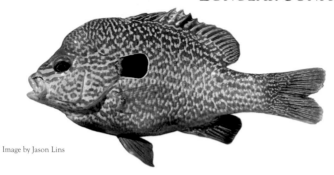

Image by Jason Lins

◆ **Description:** Longear Sunfish are named for their elongated operculum flap, which has a large ear-shaped appearance. Breeding adults can be a mottled turquoise and vermillion red. Juveniles feed on small aquatic organisms, while adults primarily feed on terrestrial insects that fall into the water.

◆ **Habitat:** Wide range of habitats. Usually found along stream banks under vegetative cover.

◆ **Range:** Southern Great Lakes and Mississippi River drainages. Historically found in embayed sections of the Little Tennessee River and in the Little Pigeon River. None have been collected in the Smokies since the 1950s, but they still exist outside the park boundary.

Lepomis megalotis
Size: 1 lb (½ kg)

REDEAR SUNFISH

Image by Grant Fisher

Lepomis microlophus

Size: Up to 4 lb (2 kg)

GREAT SMOKY MOUNTAINS
NATIONAL PARK

◆ **Description:** Also known as "Shellcrackers" due to their high consumption of snails, Redear Sunfish are easily identified by distinctive red marking near their opercular lobe. The body color is usually grayish with males developing a yellow breast during spawning. A favorite among panfish anglers, Redear Sunfish can grow up to four pounds. They feed on aquatic mollusks, insects, and crustaceans.

◆ **Habitat:** Lakes and slow-flowing backwaters of streams.

◆ **Range:** Lower Mississippi River drainage south to the Gulf of Mexico. In the Smokies, Redear Sunfish occur only along the Little Tennessee River and the lower portions of its tributaries.

LARGEMOUTH BASS

Image by Grant Fisher

◆ **Description:** The Largemouth Bass is probably the most popular sport fish in North America. It can be distinguished by a black lateral line stripe and the lack of a tooth patch on the tongue. They are often taken on minnow or crayfish lures. Stream Largemouth in the one-to-two-pound range are common, but they can reach record sizes of 20 pounds in reservoirs.

◆ **Habitat:** Slow-moving waters of larger streams and lakes.

◆ **Range:** Widespread across the United States. Rare in the park but can occasionally be found in streams of the Little Tennessee River system and in the Little Pigeon River.

Micropterus salmoides
Size: 1–2 lb (½–1 kg)

GREAT SMOKY MOUNTAINS
NATIONAL PARK

Spotted Bass

*Micropterus
punctulatus*

Size: 1–2 lb (½–1 kg)

GREAT SMOKY MOUNTAINS
NATIONAL PARK

◆ **Description:** Spotted Bass are similar in appearance to Largemouth Bass but usually have distinct red eyes and a rectangular-shaped tooth patch on their tongue. Like other bass species, Spotted Bass are sought after by anglers for the vigorous fight they provide. Adult fish in the one-to-two-pound range are fairly common. Spotted Bass feed primarily on small minnows, crayfish, and aquatic insects.
◆ **Habitat:** Found in reservoirs or slow-moving sections of large streams.
◆ **Range:** Mississippi River drainage. Spotted Bass are rare in the Smokies. Present only in the embayed areas of the Little Tennessee River.

SMALLMOUTH BASS

Image by Adam Walker

◆ **Description:** Smallmouth Bass are arguably, pound for pound, the hardest-fighting freshwater sport fish. They are differentiated from other bass species by their vertical barring color pattern, and their jaw does not extend past the eye. While they can grow to over ten pounds, Smallmouth of one-to-two pounds are commonly caught in stream ecosystems. They are predatory and feed primarily on smaller fish, crustaceans, and aquatic insects.
◆ **Habitat:** Prefers stream areas with current where rock or vegetative cover is available.
◆ **Range:** Widespread in Mississippi River drainage. Smallmouth Bass are common in the lower portions of all GSMNP rivers except those in the Pigeon River drainage.

Micropterus dolomieu
Size: 1–2 lb (½–1 kg)

GREAT SMOKY MOUNTAINS
NATIONAL PARK

WHITE CRAPPIE

Image by Grant Fisher

Pomoxis annularis
Size: Up to 5 lb (2 kg)

GREAT SMOKY MOUNTAINS
NATIONAL PARK

◆ **Description:** White Crappie closely resemble Black Crappie, but they can be distinguished by the presence of faint black vertical barring on each side of their body. Crappie are piscivorous, feeding primarily on shad and shiners, but they also consume crustaceans and plankton. They can grow to five pounds and are much sought after by anglers for their delectable meat. Females are extremely fecund and produce up to 160,000 eggs.

◆ **Habitat:** Lakes or slow-moving streams with heavy underwater cover.

◆ **Range:** Widespread across middle and eastern North America and introduced in the west. In the park, they are found in embayed areas of the Little Tennessee River.

BLACK CRAPPIE

Image by Grant Fisher

♦ **Description:** Similar in appearance to
White Crappie. Black Crappie are identified by their spotted color pattern and the
absence of vertical striping. They prefer
cooler water more so than White Crappie.
Black Crappie are also popular sport fish and
are known to feed on smaller fish as well as
crustaceans and insects.
♦ **Habitat:** Clear, cool lakes with dense
vegetative cover.
♦ **Range:** Widespread across middle and
eastern North America and introduced in the
west. In the park, they are found in embayed
areas of the Little Tennessee River.

Pomoxis
nigromaculatus
Size: Up to 3 lb (1 kg)

GREAT SMOKY MOUNTAINS
NATIONAL PARK

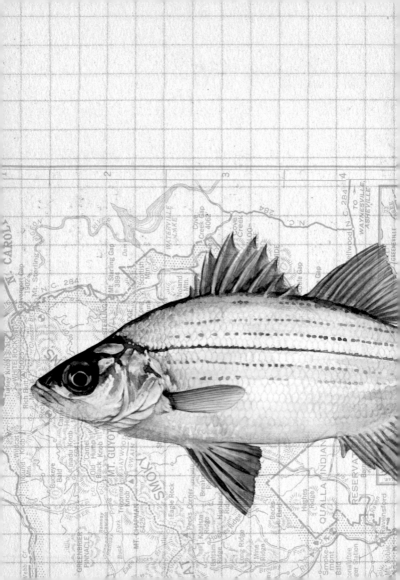

TEMPERATE BASS

Family Moronidae

White Bass

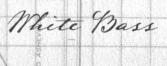

White Bass

WHITE BASS

Image by Grant Fisher

Morone chrysops
Size: Under 5 lb (2 kg)

GREAT SMOKY MOUNTAINS
NATIONAL PARK

◆ **Description:** White Bass are often mistaken for Striped Bass or Hybrid Striped Bass, but they possess several distinguishing characteristics. They are generally smaller (under five pounds) and have a single distinct lateral line running the length of their body. White Bass also have a single tooth patch, whereas Striped Bass and Hybrids have two patches. They are piscivorous, preying upon smaller fish species. White Bass are much sought after for their meat and lively fight on rod and reel.

◆ **Habitat:** Large rivers and reservoirs.

◆ **Range:** Mississippi River and Mobile River drainages. In the Smokies, White Bass are common in the Little Tennessee River system and can be found in the embayed section of Abrams Creek as well as other embayments.

N

Cane Mtn.
Crook Ridge
Look Rock
Stony Gap
CADES COVE MTN.
Abrams
Abrams Falls
C
Pine Mtn.
Andy McCully Ridge
CAI CO
Polecat Ridge
Old Mill
Tarkiln Ridge
HANNAH MOUNTAIN
Chilhowee
Panther
Creek
S
Bunker Hill
Lynn Gap
Hickory Top
GREGORY BALD 4948
Rich Gap
Chilly Spring Knob
PARSON BALD 4760'
Chuc
erwood Dam
GREAT
Shud
LDERWOOD LAKE
Deals Gap 1955
Twentymile
Creek
N. C.
NESSEE
CAROLINA
LAKE CHEOAH
Tapoca
Cheoah Dam
CHEOAH
U.S.
US 129

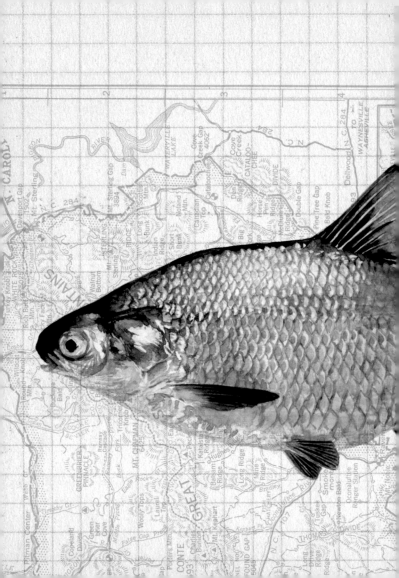

SHAD AND HERRING

Family Clupeidae

Gizzard Shad

*Gizzard
Shad*

GIZZARD SHAD

Image by Zachary Randall

Dorosoma cepedianum
Size: Up to 20 in (51 cm)

GREAT SMOKY MOUNTAINS
NATIONAL PARK

◆ **Description:** Gizzard Shad are the only fish in their family found in the Smokies. They are planktivores and feed primarily on zooplankton and phytoplankton. Gizzard Shad are often seen in large schools in reservoirs. They have extremely high populations in many lakes and reservoirs throughout the United States. While they only live three or four years, Gizzard Shad grow to 20 inches. Smaller shad are a popular baitfish and food item for predatory fish species.

◆ **Habitat:** Lakes and large rivers. Occasionally enter smaller streams.

◆ **Range:** Central and eastern drainages of North America. In GSMNP, Gizzard Shad are found in the embayed sections of Abrams Creek, Tabcat Creek, and other embayments of the Little Tennessee River.

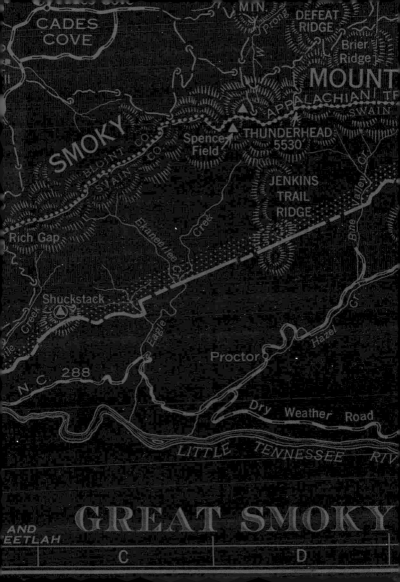

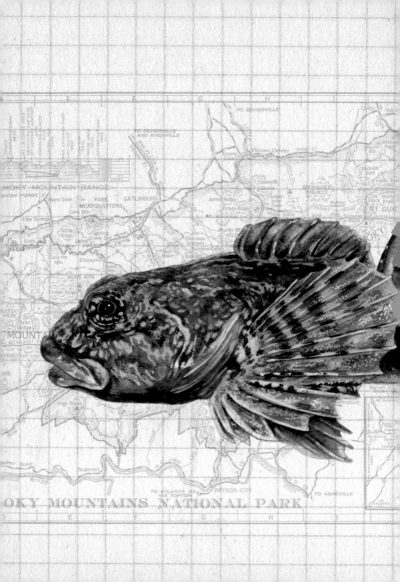

FRESHWATER SCULPINS

Family Cottidae

Mottled Sculpin

Banded Sculpin

Banded Sculpin

MOTTLED SCULPIN

Image by Adam Walker

Cottus bairdii

Size: 6 in (15 cm)

GREAT SMOKY MOUNTAINS
NATIONAL PARK

◆ **Description:** Very similar in appearance to the Banded Sculpin. The Mottled Sculpin has no gap between its dorsal fins and, ironically, lacks any mottled color pattern under its chin. Sculpin differ from many fish in that they lack a swim bladder. They remain on the stream bottom disguised by sand or small rocks and wait for prey to come along. While only reaching six inches in size, Mottled Sculpins are voracious predators and will eat anything they can swallow.

◆ **Habitat:** Somewhat variable habitat preferences. Can be found in cool, slower-flowing creeks as well as swift, high-gradient mountain streams.

◆ **Range:** Eastern North America into Canada. Mottled Sculpins are the most widespread sculpin species in the park and are common in all rivers except the Middle Prong of the Little Pigeon and Cataloochee Creek.

BANDED SCULPIN

Image by Adam Walker

♦ **Description:** Similar in appearance to the
Mottled Sculpin. Banded Sculpins can be
identified by the separation between their
dorsal fins. They also have a mottled pattern
under their chin. Banded Sculpins have no
swim bladders and use their camouflaged
pattern to ambush prey. They do grow slightly
larger than Mottled Sculpins and are also
aggressive predators.

♦ **Habitat:** Somewhat variable habitat preferences. Can be found in cool, slower-flowing
creeks as well as swift, high-gradient mountain
streams.

♦ **Range:** Found in central Mississippi River
drainages and also in Ozark and Ohio river
drainages. In the Smokies, Banded Sculpins
are common in Little River and Middle Prong
of the Little Pigeon River.

Cottus carolinae

Size: 6–7 in (15–18 cm)

GREAT SMOKY MOUNTAINS
NATIONAL PARK

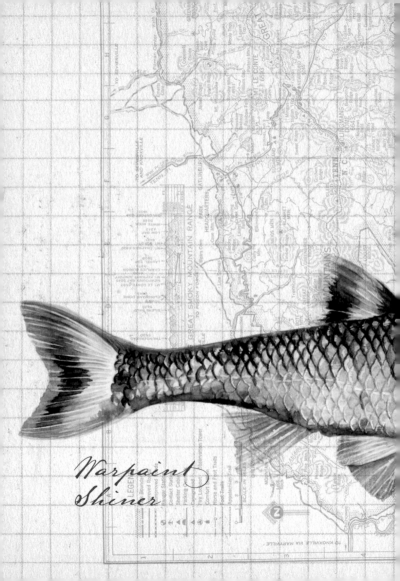

Warpaint Shiner

Minnows

Family Cyprinidae

Central Stoneroller	River Chub	Tennessee Dace
Rosyside Dace	Tennessee Shiner	Fathead Minnow
Whitetail Shiner	Silver Shiner	Eastern Blacknose Dace
Flame Chub	Saffron Shiner	Longnose Dace
Bigeye Chub	Emerald Shiner	Creek Chub
Striped Shiner	Mirror Shiner	Common Carp
Warpaint Shiner	Telescope Shiner	Goldfish
	Fatlips Minnow	

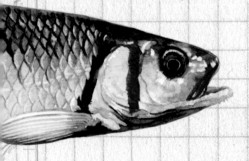

CENTRAL STONEROLLER

Image by Bryson Hilburn

*Campostoma
anomalum*

Size: 5–6 in (13–15 cm)

◆ **Description:** Male stonerollers develop hard keratinized tubercles on their head during spawning season, giving them the nickname "horny head" or "knotty." Central Stonerollers usually occur in the five-to-six-inch range and resemble other minnow species. They can be identified by their unique sucker-like mouth, which is made predominantly of cartilage and used for scraping algae off rocks while feeding. There are two verified records in the Smokies of a similar species, the Largescale Stoneroller, *Campostoma oligolepis*, but no population has ever been documented.

◆ **Habitat:** Commonly found in slower-moving water in streams of all sizes.

◆ **Range:** Widespread in eastern United States. One of the most common fish in GSMNP. Found in all streams up to 3,200 feet.

Image by Grant Fisher

◆ **Description:** As their name indicates,
Rosyside Dace have a very distinct red lateral
stripe that becomes even more vibrant during
spawning season. Growing to less than five
inches, these fish have a significantly larger
mouth than other similar minnows. Since
Rosyside Dace spawn over gravel nests, they
occasionally hybridize with other minnow species. They are surface feeders and eat primarily adult terrestrial and aquatic insects.

◆ **Habitat:** Pool areas of cold, clear streams
with rocky substrate.

◆ **Range:** Atlantic Coast drainages. In
the Smokies, Rosyside Dace are found
in the Little Tennessee River tributaries,
Oconaluftee River, and upper Abrams Creek
in Cades Cove.

Clinostomus
funduloides

Size: Up to 5 in (13 cm)

GREAT SMOKY MOUNTAINS
NATIONAL PARK

WHITETAIL SHINER

Image by Adam Walker

Cyprinella galactura

Size: Up to 6 in (15 cm)

GREAT SMOKY MOUNTAINS
NATIONAL PARK

◆ **Description:** The Whitetail Shiner is recognized by its silvery pattern and white-colored fins. Breeding males can develop light orange fin tips along with keratinous breeding tubercles. Whitetail Shiners are one of the larger shiners found in the park and can grow to six inches. Sometimes caught on small flies, they typically feed on terrestrial insects or drifting aquatic insect larvae.

◆ **Habitat:** Prefer swifter-flowing runs or pools.

◆ **Range:** Cumberland and Tennessee River drainages and south to Savannah River drainage with a separate population in Arkansas. Common in all lower portions of major Smokies streams except those in the Pigeon River drainage.

Image by Bernard Kuhajda

◆ **Description:** Flame Chubs are named for the fiery red coloration found on breeding males. They differ from many fish in that they are inhabitants of spring-influenced waters with lots of aquatic vegetation. The Flame Chub feeds mostly on aquatic midge larvae, along with snails, isopods, and filamentous green algae. They rarely grow to more than three inches.

◆ **Habitat:** Well-vegetated spring-fed waters.

◆ **Range:** Tennessee, upper Duck, and middle Cumberland river systems. Flame Chubs are very rare in the Smokies and only found in spring-fed pools in Cades Cove.

Hemitremia flammea
Size: 3 in (8 cm)

GREAT SMOKY MOUNTAINS
NATIONAL PARK

BIGEYE CHUB

Image by Adam Walker

Hybopsis amblops
Size: 4 in (10 cm)

◆ **Description:** Bigeye Chubs are similar in appearance to many shiner species in the genus *Notropis* but have very large eyes and a more downward-facing, subterminal mouth. The Latin word *amblops* translates to "blunt face." The black lateral line can be faint in some adults. The Bigeye Chub's diet consists mostly of stonefly and mayfly larvae.

◆ **Habitat:** Sandy or silty areas with moderate flow.

◆ **Range:** Southern Great Lakes and Mississippi River drainages. In the park, Bigeye Chubs are fairly common in lower portions of Little River, Tabcat Creek, and Abrams Creek.

Image by Grant Fisher

♦ **Description:** Striped Shiners are recognized by their basic silvery color and the large tubercles on breeding males. Male fish undergo a noticeable change during spawning when their silver color blends with light yellow-orange areas and fin tips become pink or red. Males also develop a deep-bodied appearance. Striped Shiners are aggressive feeders and thrive off large insects and small crayfish.

♦ **Habitat:** Prefers pool areas of streams with gravel substrate.

♦ **Range:** Southern Great Lakes and Mississippi River drainages. In GSMNP, Striped Shiners are only found in the lower portions of Abrams Creek. They occur in Little River and the Little Pigeon River but outside the park boundary.

Luxilus chrysocephalus
Size: Up to 9 in (23 cm)

GREAT SMOKY MOUNTAINS
NATIONAL PARK

WARPAINT SHINER

Image by Adam Walker

Luxilus coccogenis

Size: Up to 5 in (13 cm)

GREAT SMOKY MOUNTAINS
NATIONAL PARK

◆ **Description:** Warpaint Shiners are a large species of shiner easily recognized by the orange "warpaint" markings around their gills, dorsal fin, and mouth. They are very tolerant of cold water and are occasionally caught by anglers. Like other minnow species, Warpaint Shiners use chub nests as spawning areas. They feed on drifting aquatic or terrestrial insects.

◆ **Habitat:** Moderate-to-swift flow areas of clear, cool streams with rocky substrate.

◆ **Range:** Common in the Blue Ridge region of Tennessee and found throughout the Carolinas. They are found in all Smokies streams up to 2,200 feet except those in the Pigeon River drainage.

Image by Adam Walker

♦ **Description:** River Chubs are a minnow species known for the large keratinous breeding tubercles found on males. Like the Central Stoneroller, River Chubs are often referred to as "knotty" or "horny heads" and sometimes caught by anglers. They build large gravel piles in streams during spawning by carrying one stone at a time. This action is key in the facilitation of other minnow species spawning as well. River Chubs feed upon all types of aquatic insects and small crustaceans.

♦ **Habitat:** Larger creeks with high current and rocky substrate.

♦ **Range:** Great Lakes, Upper Tennessee, Cumberland, and Ohio river drainages. River Chubs are widespread in all park stream systems up to 2,800 feet except those in the Pigeon River drainage.

Nocomis micropogon

Size: 10-12 in
(25-30 cm)

GREAT SMOKY MOUNTAINS
NATIONAL PARK

TENNESSEE SHINER

Image by Adam Walker

Notropis leuciodus

Size: 3½ in (9 cm)

GREAT SMOKY MOUNTAINS
NATIONAL PARK

◆ **Description:** Tennessee Shiners are very common and similar in appearance to other shiners in the genus *Notropis*. During spawning, however, males become a brilliant red color and can often be seen schooling over chub nests. Another way to identify Tennessee Shiners is the presence of a black rectangular mark at the base of the caudal fin. They are one of the smaller shiner species and only grow to three and a half inches. Other than spawning behavior, much of the Tennessee Shiner's biology is unknown.

◆ **Habitat:** Pool areas of bedrock or boulder streams.

◆ **Range:** Tennessee and Cumberland river drainages. Common in all Smokies streams up to 2,200 feet except those in the Pigeon River drainage.

Image by Bernard Kuhajda

◆ **Description:** The Silver Shiner is named for its silver coloration. It has a long, slender body and fins that are clear white. Silver Shiners possess an upturned mouth, since they are surface feeders, and have two dark crescent shapes between the nostrils. They can often be seen jumping out of the water after prey.

◆ **Habitat:** Pools of clear streams.

◆ **Range:** Lake Erie tributaries, south to Ohio, Cumberland, and Tennessee river drainages. Silver Shiners are rare in the Smokies but sometimes found in lower portions of Little River, Oconaluftee River, and tributaries of the Little Tennessee River.

Notropis photogenis
Size: 6 in (15 cm)

SAFFRON SHINER

Image by Adam Walker

Notropis rubricroceus

Size: Up to 3½ in (9 cm)

GREAT SMOKY MOUNTAINS
NATIONAL PARK

◆ **Description:** The easiest way to identify a Saffron Shiner is to look for the presence of red "lipstick" markings around the mouth. During spawning, males will develop bright red colors around their head and lower body. Their fins can have a yellowish tint as well. They often spawn in schools over chub nests. Saffron Shiners can live up to five years.

◆ **Habitat:** Cool, clear trout streams with moderate flow.

◆ **Range:** Upper Tennessee River drainage south to Little Tennessee River. In the Smokies, they are found in Little River, Little Pigeon River, and Cosby Creek. They are rarely seen in Mill Creek in Cades Cove.

EMERALD SHINER

Image courtesy US Fish and Wildlife Services

◆ **Description:** Emerald Shiners have a slender appearance with a silver color pattern. Some possess a light silver or greenish dorsal coloration. The dorsal fin is set farther back than other shiners, which makes the Emerald Shiner resemble Brook Silversides. They are nighttime spawners and feed on zooplankton and midge larvae. Emerald Shiners are sometimes sold as baitfish in tackle stores. Adults grow to five inches.

◆ **Habitat:** Found in lakes, reservoirs, big rivers, and the mouths of small creeks.

◆ **Range:** Widespread in the Mississippi River drainage. In the park, they are found near the mouth of Abrams Creek in the embayed area of the Little Tennessee River.

Notropis atherinoides
Size: Up to 5 in (13 cm)

GREAT SMOKY MOUNTAINS
NATIONAL PARK

MIRROR SHINER

Image courtesy US Geological Survey

Notropis spectrunculus

Size: Up to 3 in (8 cm)

◆ **Description:** The Mirror Shiner is similar in appearance to the Tennessee Shiner, but it has a blunter nose and a black triangular-shaped mark on the caudal fin base. Breeding males develop orange coloration near the pectoral and dorsal fins. The biology of the Mirror Shiner is largely unknown.

◆ **Habitat:** Rocky pools and runs.

◆ **Range:** Upper Tennessee River system. In the Smokies, Mirror Shiners are found in the Oconaluftee River and tributaries of the Little Tennessee River.

TELESCOPE SHINER

Image by Adam Walker

◆ **Description:** Telescope Shiners are often mistaken for Tennessee Shiners due to their similar appearance and distribution. However, Telescope Shiners do not have the black rectangular mark at the base of their caudal fin and have much larger eyes. They also do not have bright breeding colors. Food sources include a mix of terrestrial and aquatic insects.

◆ **Habitat:** Areas adjacent to riffles in rocky streams.

◆ **Range:** Tennessee and Cumberland river drainages. In the Smokies, Telescope Shiners are common in Abrams Creek, Little River, and the Little Pigeon River.

Notropis telescopus

Size: Up to 4½ in (12 cm)

GREAT SMOKY MOUNTAINS
NATIONAL PARK

FATLIPS MINNOW

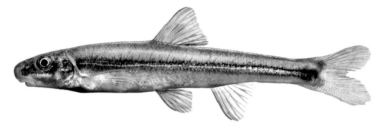

Image courtesy of ncfishes.com

Phenacobius crassilabrum

Size: Up to 4½ in (12 cm)

GREAT SMOKY MOUNTAINS
NATIONAL PARK

◆ **Description:** Fatlips Minnows are similar in appearance to some chub species but have a unique sucker-like mouth and prominent black lateral stripe. They are not very long-lived and rarely survive more than three years. The Fatlips Minnow feeds primarily on midge and crane fly larvae.

◆ **Habitat:** Riffle areas of cold trout streams.

◆ **Range:** Upper Tennessee River drainage from the Holston to Little Tennessee River. Fatlips Minnows are rare in the Smokies and only found in the Oconaluftee River.

TENNESSEE DACE

Image by Shawna Fix

◆ **Description:** Tennessee Dace are identified by the bright red coloration seen on breeding males. Both males and females have a silver lateral stripe. They are omnivores and consume both aquatic vegetation and macroinvertebrate larvae. The Tennessee Dace is currently listed as vulnerable by the International Union for Conservation of Nature.

◆ **Habitat:** Shallow pools in low-gradient streams.

◆ **Range:** Only occurs in certain areas of Tennessee's Blue Ridge and Ridge and Valley provinces. In the Smokies, Tennessee Dace are rarely found in lower Tabcat Creek and Cosby Creek.

Chrosomus tennesseensis

Size: Up to 3 in (8 cm)

GREAT SMOKY MOUNTAINS
NATIONAL PARK

Fathead Minnow

Image courtesy of ncfishes.com

Pimephales promelas
Size: Up to 3 in (8 cm)

◆ **Description:** While rarely seen in the Smokies, Fathead Minnows are a popular baitfish and often discarded by anglers—thus, one reason the National Park Service does not allow live bait to be used. Fathead Minnows resemble Creek Chubs in appearance but change drastically during spawning. Males develop a large dark head and keratinized breeding tubercles. They are omnivorous fish and thrive on a mixture of aquatic insects and plant material.

◆ **Habitat:** Slow-flowing areas of warm-water streams.

◆ **Range:** Wide ranging throughout the United States into Canada. In the Smokies, Fathead Minnows can be found only in the lower portions of Little River and the embayed sections of the Little Tennessee River.

EASTERN BLACKNOSE DACE

Image by Adam Walker

◆ **Description:** Eastern Blacknose Dace are a
very common fish species that can be found
near the headwaters of streams. They can be
identified by the distinct black line that runs
from their eye to nose. They can also have
some black speckling on their sides. Breeding
males develop orange coloration on their
lower body. Eastern Blacknose Dace feed on a
variety of aquatic invertebrates. Their typical
life span is three to four years.

◆ **Habitat:** Shallow areas with moderate
current.

◆ **Range:** Mississippi and upper Mobile river
drainages. In GSMNP, Eastern Blacknose
Dace are found in Abrams Creek and the
Little River and Little Pigeon River systems up
to 4,000 feet.

Rhinichthys atratulus
Size: Up to 5 in (13 cm)

Longnose Dace

Image by Adam Walker

Rhinichthys cataractae

Size: Up to 7 in (18 cm)

◆ **Description:** Longnose Dace grow larger than Eastern Blacknose Dace and have a downward-pointing, subterminal mouth. They generally have a flatter, more stream-lined body shape. Their fins can also have a red tint to them. Longnose Dace primarily feed on mayfly, blackfly, and midge larvae.
◆ **Habitat:** Swift riffle areas of cold-water streams.
◆ **Range:** Upper Tennessee River drainage, north to Canada and west to Pacific Basin. In the Smokies, they are found up to 3,200 feet in upper Little River, tributaries of the Little Tennessee River, and the Oconaluftee River.

CREEK CHUB

Image by Adam Walker

◆ **Description:** Creek Chubs can be easily identified by the black spot on the base of their dorsal fin. They also have a black lateral line stripe running the length of their body. Similar to River Chubs, Creek Chubs also build pebble nests one rock at a time. Females can produce as many as 7,500 eggs per year. Creek Chubs usually feed on fallen terrestrial insects and live up to six years. They are often caught by anglers.

◆ **Habitat:** Pool areas with plenty of vegetative cover.

◆ **Range:** Found throughout eastern North America and the Midwest. In the Smokies, Creek Chubs can be found in the Little Pigeon River, Little River, Oconaluftee River, Tabcat Creek, and upper Abrams Creek.

Semotilus atromaculatus

Size: Up to 12 in (31 cm)

GREAT SMOKY MOUNTAINS
NATIONAL PARK

COMMON CARP

Image by Dave Neely

Cyprinus carpio

Size: Can grow to over
100 lb (45 kg)

◆ **Description:** Common Carp were first introduced to North America in the 1800s as a food fish for the fast-growing nation. They reproduced in such great numbers that native fish populations began to suffer. Carp are very tolerant to pollution and can live in dirty water with little dissolved oxygen. They feed by rooting through the substrate and consuming insect larvae, plankton, and aquatic vegetation. Common Carp are a golden-brown color with noticeable barbels or "whiskers" at the corners of their mouths.

◆ **Habitat:** Large rivers and reservoirs.

◆ **Range:** Native to Europe and Asia and widespread in Canada, North America, and Mexico. In the Smokies, Common Carp can be found in the embayed areas of the Little Tennessee River.

GOLDFISH

Image by Noah Daun

Carassius auratus
Size: Up to 2 ft (61 cm)

♦ **Description:** Taxonomically, Goldfish are considered the same species as the popular aquarium pet. They were originally imported from areas in Europe and Asia and selectively bred for the aquarium trade. Many variations of Goldfish exist, and a number of them have been introduced into the wild. Young wild Goldfish are often sold as bait labeled "Baltimore Minnows." Goldfish have a similar appearance to Common Carp but have 25 to 31 lateral line scales. Most have a golden coloration, but orange varieties also exist. They feed on aquatic insects, detritus, and vegetation. In the wild, they can grow to nearly two feet.

♦ **Habitat:** Large rivers, lakes, and ponds.

♦ **Range:** Native to Europe and Asia but widely introduced in the United States and Canada. Goldfish can be found in embayed areas of the Little Tennessee River in the Smokies.

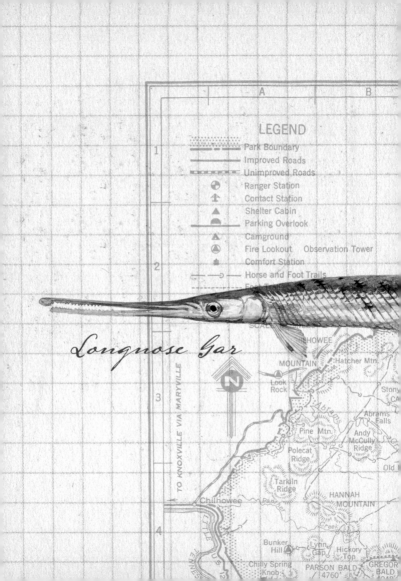

LEGEND

━ ━ ━ Park Boundary
━━━━ Improved Roads
▪▪▪▪▪ Unimproved Roads
◉ Ranger Station
⛨ Contact Station
▲ Shelter Cabin
▲ Parking Overlook
▲ Campground
◉ Fire Lookout   Observation Tower
🏠 Comfort Station
━ ━o━ Horse and Foot Trails
▪▪▪▪▪ Foot Tr

Longnose Gar

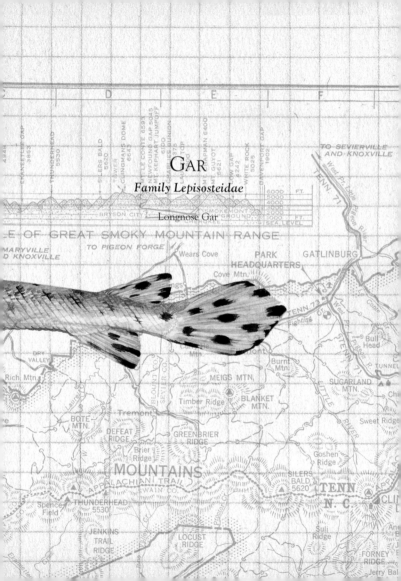

GAR

Family Lepisosteidae

Longnose Gar

LONGNOSE GAR

Image by Dave Neely

Lepisosteus osseus
Size: Over 6 ft (183 cm)

GREAT SMOKY MOUNTAINS
NATIONAL PARK

◆ **Description:** An ancient and primitive fish, the Longnose Gar is easily recognized by its long mouth, array of pointed teeth, and armored scales. They can grow quite large (over 6 feet and 50 pounds), which seems alarming to some. However, they only feed on small fish. Longnose Gar have an extremely elongated and narrow mouth specifically adapted to snatching smaller fish species like shad or minnows. They are the most common of the four gar species. A common method of catching Longnose Gar is to use a frayed rope lure, which tangles in the fish's mouth and needs no hook. It is important to note that the eggs of Longnose Gar are toxic to humans.

◆ **Habitat:** Large rivers, swamps, and reservoirs. Longnose Gar prefer slower-moving water.

◆ **Range:** Mississippi River drainage and the Southeast. In the Smokies, Longnose Gar are occasionally found in the lower portions of Little Tennessee River tributaries.

Legend:
- ⊸— Horse and Foot Trails
- ------- Foot Trails
- ••••••••• Appalachian Trail

SCALE IN MILES
0 1 2 3 4 5 6

N

Kinzel Spr
Hurricane Mtn

CHILHOWEE

Hatcher Mtn.

Beard
Cane
Mtn.

Crooked
Ridge

MOUNTAIN

Look
Rock

Stony Gap

CADES COVE
MTN.

Abrams

Abrams
Falls

Cad

Pine Mtn.

Andy
McCully
Ridge

CADE
COV

Polecat
Ridge

Old Mill

Tarkiln
Ridge

HANNAH

MOUNTAIN

lhowee

Panther

SM

Creek

Bunker
Hill

Lynn
Gap

Hickory
Top

Rich Gap

Chilly Spring
Knob

PARSON BALD
4760'

GREGORY
BALD
4948

GREAT

129

ood Dam

Shucks

RWOOD LAKE

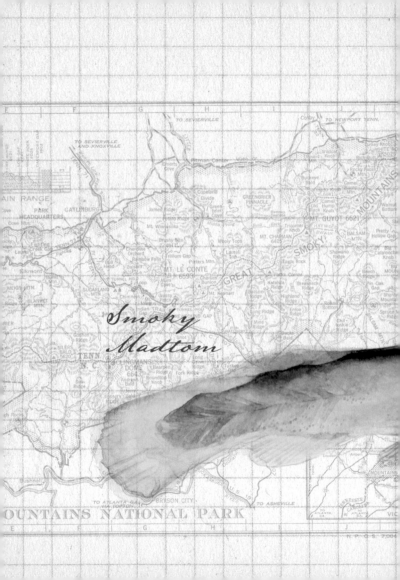

Smoky
Madtom

CATFISH
Family Ictaluridae

Yellow Bullhead

Black Bullhead

Smoky Madtom

Yellowfin Madtom

Flathead Catfish

Blue Catfish

Channel Catfish

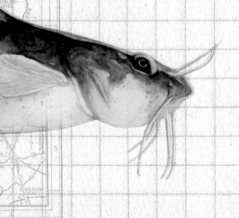

YELLOW BULLHEAD

Ameiurus natalis

Size: Up to 2 lb (1 kg)

GREAT SMOKY MOUNTAINS
NATIONAL PARK

◆ **Description:** Out of the three bullhead species found in North America, the Yellow Bullhead is the easiest to distinguish. It is the only species of bullhead with white chin barbels, or "whiskers." Black and Brown bullhead both possess dark chin barbels. Yellow Bullhead can live up to seven years and weigh several pounds. While smaller than other catfish, Yellow Bullhead are quite gluttonous and will consume any available insect, crustacean, or smaller fish.

◆ **Habitat:** Found in all habitats but prefer still pools.

◆ **Range:** Widespread throughout the Midwest and eastern North America. In the Smokies, Yellow Bullhead are found in the embayed areas of Abrams Creek and Tabcat Creek along the Little Tennessee River.

BLACK BULLHEAD

Image courtesy of ncfishes.com

◆ **Description:** Black Bullhead look similar to Yellow Bullhead but with a few differences. The most obvious characteristics are their black barbels, dark brown-to-black coloration, and yellow-white belly. Like other catfish species, they are not picky about food and thrive on a variety of aquatic insects, snails, fingernail clams, and small fish. Typical Black Bullhead are rather small, but they can grow to eight pounds.

◆ **Habitat:** Still waters of lakes, ponds, and streams.

◆ **Range:** Widespread in the Mississippi River system. In the Smokies, Black Bullhead are found in the lowest portions of Abrams Creek and reservoirs of the Little Tennessee River.

Ameiurus melas
Size: Up to 8 lb (4 kg)

GREAT SMOKY MOUNTAINS
NATIONAL PARK

SMOKY MADTOM

Image by Conservation Fisheries Inc.

Noturus baileyi

Size: Up to 3 in (8 cm)

GREAT SMOKY MOUNTAINS
NATIONAL PARK

◆ **Description:** The Smoky Madtom was originally extirpated from Abrams Creek in 1957, when all nongame fish species were eliminated for the purpose of improving the trout fishery. Since then, the National Park Service has collaborated with the nonprofit organization Conservation Fisheries to rear and reintroduce Smoky Madtoms back into Abrams Creek. While current populations are well established, the Smoky Madtom is still listed as a federally endangered fish species. They reproduce by nesting underneath rocks in the stream. It is vital to their survival that park visitors do not move rocks. Smoky Madtoms are similar in appearance to Yellowfin Madtoms but are a darker grayish-brown color and have a dark bar on their adipose fin. They feed on aquatic insects.

◆ **Habitat:** Transitional areas between riffles and pools. Prefers hiding under large, flat rocks.

◆ **Range:** Smoky Madtoms are found only in lower Abrams Creek in the Smokies and Citico Creek in the Cherokee National Forest. They are found nowhere else in the world.

YELLOWFIN MADTOM

Image by Conservation Fisheries Inc.

◆ **Description:** Currently listed as a federally threatened species, the Yellowfin Madtom shares many similarities with the Smoky Madtom. They have a sandy yellow coloration and dark blotch at the base of their dorsal fin. Yellowfin Madtoms have similar nesting behavior to Smoky Madtoms and were originally extirpated from Abrams Creek in the Smokies until their reintroduction. National Park Service biologists continue to collaborate with Conservation Fisheries in the monitoring of this species. Yellowfin Madtoms grow slightly larger than Smoky Madtoms at five inches and can live up to four years. They feed at nighttime on aquatic insects.

◆ **Habitat:** Slower-moving sections of stream. Hides under rocks.

◆ **Range:** Select rivers in East Tennessee north to Virginia. In the Smokies, they are only found in the lower section of Abrams Creek.

Noturus flavipinnis
Size: 5 in (13 cm)

GREAT SMOKY MOUNTAINS
NATIONAL PARK

FLATHEAD CATFISH

Pylodictis olivaris

Size: Up to 100 lb (45 kg)

GREAT SMOKY MOUNTAINS
NATIONAL PARK

◆ **Description:** Flathead Catfish get their name from having a compressed head and wide mouth. They are inhabitants of reservoirs and large river systems. Like other catfish species, Flathead Catfish are known to feed at night. They are unique in the fact that they are more active hunters than Blue or Channel Catfish and are occasionally caught on artificial lures. Typical food items are smaller fish species. Flathead catfish can grow to very large sizes (up to 100 pounds) and live 20 years.

◆ **Habitat:** Heavy cover areas or caves in reservoirs.

◆ **Range:** Common in the central United States, south to Mexico. The Smokies are on the eastern portion of its range. Flathead Catfish can be found in reservoirs of the Tennessee River.

BLUE CATFISH

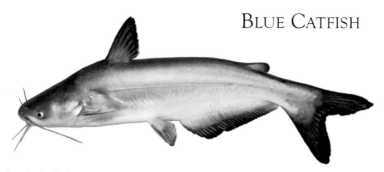

Image by Dave Neely

◆ **Description:** Blue Catfish are the largest member of their family in North America. They can be identified by their grayish-blue coloration and pale underside. The anal fin is also more squared off than other catfish species. Blue Catfish are often targeted by anglers hoping to land the next lunker. Surviving on a diet of fish, crustaceans, and fingernail and Asian clams, Blue Catfish can grow over five feet and weigh more than 150 pounds. They are often caught using cut pieces of shad or Skipjack.

◆ **Habitat:** Deep channels of large rivers and reservoirs.

◆ **Range:** Mississippi River drainage to Gulf of Mexico. Blue Catfish are rare in the Smokies and can be found in the reservoirs of the Little Tennessee River and can enter embayed areas such as Abrams Creek.

Ictalurus furcatus

Size: Can weigh more than 150 lb (68 kg)

GREAT SMOKY MOUNTAINS
NATIONAL PARK

CHANNEL CATFISH

Image by Dave Neely

Ictalurus punctatus

Size: Can grow to over
50 lb (23 kg)

◆ **Description:** Channel Catfish are the most commonly occurring catfish species in North America. Their color ranges from gray to olive brown, and many often have scattered black lateral spotting. Like other catfish species, Channel Catfish do most of their feeding at night and prefer to shelter in cover during the day. Anglers target Channel Catfish for the vigorous fight and excellent quality meat. Cut bait, worms, or scented baits are often used. Channel Catfish eat other fish primarily but also consume crustaceans and mollusks.

◆ **Habitat:** Deep pools of moderate-to-large rivers and reservoirs. They are stocked in ponds.

◆ **Range:** Widespread in United States into Canada. Channel Catfish are common in the Little Tennessee River reservoirs and embayed areas of Smokies streams.

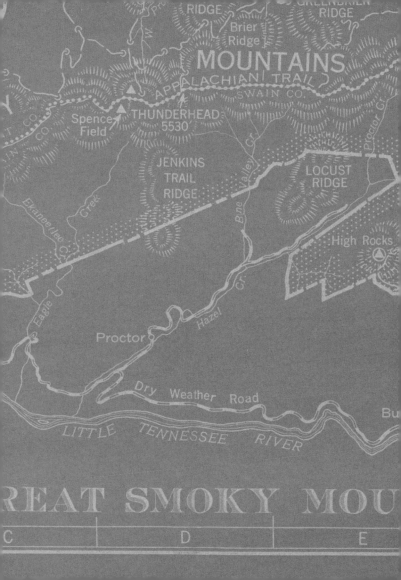

Tangerine
Darter

DARTERS, PERCH, AND WALLEYE
Family Percidae

Greenside Darter	Wounded Darter
Greenfin Darter	Banded Darter
Fantail Darter	Yellow Perch
Tuckasegee Darter	Tangerine Darter
Blueside Darter	Logperch
Citico Darter	Gilt Darter
Redline Darter	Olive Darter
Tennessee Snubnose Darter	Walleye
Swannanoa Darter	Sauger

GREENSIDE DARTER

Image by Adam Walker

*Etheostoma
blennioides*

Size: Up to 6½ in
(17 cm)

GREAT SMOKY MOUNTAINS
NATIONAL PARK

◆ **Description:** Greenside Darters can be
most easily distinguished by their six to seven
U-shaped lateral markings. They also have
a downward-oriented, subterminal mouth.
Greensides are the largest darter in the
Etheostoma genus, reaching a maximum size
of six and a half inches and living five years.
Their diet is composed mostly of mayfly and
caddisfly larvae.

◆ **Habitat:** Swift riffle habitat with cobble or
boulder substrate.

◆ **Range:** Tennessee and Ohio river drainages. In the Smokies, Greenside Darters are
common in all park stream systems except
those in the Pigeon River.

Image by Adam Walker

◆ **Description:** Not to be confused with the Greenside Darter, the Greenfin Darter has a completely different appearance. While possessing a terminal mouth and thick body, it also sports a very dark green (almost black) color. Breeding males have richly colored green fins, while females are a dull olive color. Greenfin Darters have an extremely diverse diet. Gut analyses have shown that they consume 10 to 15 different taxa of aquatic invertebrates. They can live as long as five years.

◆ **Habitat:** Cold-water streams with bedrock or boulder substrates.

◆ **Range:** Blue Ridge sections of the Upper Tennessee River drainage. In the park, Greenfin Darters are common in the Little Pigeon River, Abrams Creek, and Oconaluftee River.

Etheostoma chlorobranchium

Size: Up to 4 in (10 cm)

GREAT SMOKY MOUNTAINS
NATIONAL PARK

FANTAIL DARTER

Image by Adam Walker

Etheostoma flabellare

Size: Up to 3 in (8 cm)

◆ **Description:** Characteristics of the Fantail Darter include a robust caudal fin, which is a translucent yellow with black speckles, and a unique first dorsal fin, which contains seven to eight gold knobs at each spine tip. A smaller darter, the Fantail only grows to around three inches. They consume a variety of aquatic insects. Fantail Darters have an interesting nesting behavior. They nest in rock cavities, and the male will chase away the female once she lays eggs and proceed to guard them alone until hatching. Due to its specific nesting and clean water requirements, the Fantail Darter is a sensitive species that is highly susceptible to human disturbance.

◆ **Habitat:** Fast-flowing, shallow riffles.

◆ **Range:** Great Lakes drainage and south to Tennessee and North Carolina. Found in the Little Pigeon River and Abrams Creek in the park. Also found in the Little River just outside the park.

Image by Adam Walker

Etheostoma gutselli
Size: Up to 6½ in (17 cm)

GREAT SMOKY MOUNTAINS
NATIONAL PARK

◆ **Description:** Tuckasegee Darters appear similar to Greenside Darters, but their fins typically have more of an orange color, and the U-shaped marks are not as distinct. Biologically, they are similar to Greenside Darters in size, life span, and diet preferences. They used to be considered a subspecies of Greenside Darters but have recently been elevated to species level.

◆ **Habitat:** Swift riffle habitat with cobble or boulder substrate.

◆ **Range:** Found only in the Pigeon and Little Tennessee river systems. In the Smokies, Tuckasegee Darters are found in the Oconaluftee River as well as streams draining to embayed areas of the Little Tennessee River.

BLUESIDE DARTER

Image by Jason Lins

Etheostoma jessiae

Size: Up to 3 in (8 cm)

◆ **Description:** Blueside Darters are a member of the Speckled Darter complex (a taxonomic grouping), and they can be identified by the bright blue coloration around their gills and blue lateral stripes developed during spawning. Rarely ever reaching three years of age, Blueside Darters are quite short-lived. They feed primarily on chironomid midge larvae. Little else is known about their biology.

◆ **Habitat:** Sluggish areas of stream with fine gravel or sandy substrate.

◆ **Range:** Tennessee and Holston river systems. In the Smokies, they were historically found in lower Abrams Creek. They can still be found in the West Prong of the Little Pigeon River outside the park boundary.

Image by Grant Fisher

◆ **Description:** Taxonomically, the Citico Darter is one of four new species split from the Duskytail Darter in 2008. It was originally found in lower Abrams Creek but was eliminated in 1957 during an attempt to improve the trout fishery. Due to the collaboration between National Park Service staff and Conservation Fisheries, the restoration of the Citico Darter has had great success, but the species is still considered federally endangered by the US Fish and Wildlife Service. All four new species are federally endangered but under the single Duskytail Darter name. This includes Citico, Marbled, Tuxedo, and Duskytail darters. Yearly snorkel surveys of Abrams Creek are conducted to monitor the populations. Citico Darters can be easily identified by their dark bronze or brown color and six to seven gold knobs at the tip of each spine on the first dorsal fin. Males guard the nest, and like other darters, they feed on aquatic insects.

Etheostoma sitikuense
Size: Up to 3 in (8 cm)

GREAT SMOKY MOUNTAINS NATIONAL PARK

◆ **Habitat:** Slow-flowing areas near riffles. Prefers hiding under large, flat rocks.
◆ **Range:** Only found in Abrams Creek in the Smokies. Also found in Citico Creek and the Tellico River.

REDLINE DARTER

Image by Adam Walker

Etheostoma rufilineatum
Size: Up to 4 in (10 cm)

GREAT SMOKY MOUNTAINS
NATIONAL PARK

◆ **Description:** As one of the most colorful fish in the Smokies, the Redline Darter can be identified by the vibrant red color and checkerboard pattern males develop during spawning. Some Redline Darters, however, have an extreme variation in their color. Some are brightly colored, while others take on a dark olive coloration. Other identifying marks include two horizontal marks under each eye and two light yellow marks at the base of the caudal fin. Redline Darters primarily feed on mayfly and caddisfly larvae along with water mites. They can live as long as four years.

◆ **Habitat:** Fast-flowing riffles of clear streams.

◆ **Range:** Tennessee and Cumberland River drainages. They are commonly found in the Little Pigeon River, Little River, and Abrams and Tabcat creeks of the Little Tennessee River system in the Smokies.

TENNESSEE SNUBNOSE DARTER

Image by Adam Walker

◆ **Description:** The Tennessee Snubnose Darter is one of the most common darters in Great Smoky Mountains National Park. It is easily identified by its distinctive rounded snout. They also possess a vertical bar directly below the eye. Like other darters, Tennessee Snubnose Darters do not have a swim bladder, since they are uniquely adapted to live along the stream bottom. They feed on small aquatic invertebrates.

◆ **Habitat:** Riffle and run areas of small to moderate-sized streams.

◆ **Range:** Tennessee and Cumberland River drainages. In the Smokies, Tennessee Snubnose Darters are found in the Little Pigeon River, Little River, Abrams Creek, the Tabcat Creek area of the Little Tennessee River, and Cosby Creek drainage in the Pigeon River.

Etheostoma simoterum
Size: Up to 3 in (8 cm)

SWANNANOA DARTER

Image by Adam Walker

Etheostoma swannanoa

Size: Up to 4 in (10 cm)

GREAT SMOKY MOUNTAINS
NATIONAL PARK

◆ **Description:** Swannanoa Darters bear somewhat of a resemblance to the Greenside Darter. They have a subterminal mouth and nine to eleven black lateral blotches. Generally, Swannanoa Darters have a tan base color, and males develop bright blue coloration along their bottom fins. Breeding males also have orange spotting along each side of their body. The remaining biological aspects of the Swannanoa Darter are unstudied.

◆ **Habitat:** Clear streams with boulder substrate.

◆ **Range:** Upper Tennessee River system. Swannanoa Darters are found in the Little Pigeon River, Cosby Creek, and Big Creek areas of the Smokies.

Image by Adam Walker

◆ **Description:** Wounded Darters are named for their "wounds," which appear as bright red spots that occur laterally on each side. Their bodies are usually an olive color. Approximately eight very faint vertical bands are visible along each side as well. Wounded Darters are extremely territorial of their nests, and males guard them until all eggs hatch. They feed mostly on chironomid midge larvae but consume other aquatic insects as well. Wounded darters can live for up to five years.

◆ **Habitat:** Moderate-sized streams with boulder substrate.

◆ **Range:** Upper Tennessee River system. In GSMNP, Wounded Darters are found in lower Little River, lower Abrams Creek, Middle Prong of the Little Pigeon River, and the Oconaluftee River.

Etheostoma vulneratum
Size: 3½ in (9 cm)

GREAT SMOKY MOUNTAINS
NATIONAL PARK

BANDED DARTER

Image by Adam Walker

Etheostoma zonale

Size: Up to 3 in (8 cm)

GREAT SMOKY MOUNTAINS
NATIONAL PARK

◆ **Description:** While Banded Darters are relatively small darters at three inches, they can be easily identified by their distinctive vertical green bars. Male Banded Darters develop rich green coloration around their mouth, lower body, and first dorsal fin during spawning season. Females attach their eggs to vegetation in riffle areas. Banded Darters feed primarily on blackfly and mayfly larvae.

◆ **Habitat:** Riffle areas of streams with gravel and vegetation.

◆ **Range:** Ohio, Cumberland, Tennessee, and Mississippi River drainages. Introduced and established in Alabama and Georgia. In the Smokies, they are found in lower Abrams Creek and in Little River and Tuckasegee River outside the park boundary.

Image by Jason Lins

◆ **Description:** Yellow Perch are a popular sport fish in northern regions, and many consider it to be one of the best tasting fish. They can be identified by their unique stream-lined body shape as well as by the six faint vertical lateral bars. Yellow Perch are considered predators, eating insects and any available smaller fish. Anglers often catch them on soft plastics or small crankbaits. Yellow Perch are a relatively small game fish, with most being under a pound, but they can grow to several pounds if conditions are right. They are often accidentally introduced when stocking Walleye.

Perca flavescens

Size: Most are under 1 lb (½ kg)

◆ **Habitat:** Cool reservoirs and run and pool areas of streams.
◆ **Range:** Native to Canada and northern United States. They are widely introduced elsewhere including the Smokies and found along the tributaries of the Little Tennessee River. Yellow Perch are also found in the Little River outside the park boundary.

TANGERINE DARTER

Image by Bryson Hilburn

Percina aurantiaca

Size: Up to 7 in (18 cm)

GREAT SMOKY MOUNTAINS
NATIONAL PARK

◆ **Description:** The Tangerine Darter is another one of the park's colorful darters and can be easily identified by the bright yellow or orange color that breeding males develop. Dominant males have brighter colors and spawn more frequently than nondominant males, but they do not defend their territories. Females have a paler coloration. Growing to a size of seven inches, Tangerine Darters are the largest darter species in the Smokies. They are also occasionally caught by anglers. Their typical life span is four years, and their primary food source is caddisfly larvae.

◆ **Habitat:** Deeper riffles and runs of large streams with bedrock or boulder substrate.

◆ **Range:** Upper Tennessee River drainage. Tangerine Darters are found in the Little River and sections of the Little Pigeon River outside the park. They are rare in the Little Tennessee River system.

Image by Matthew Butzin

◆ **Description:** Logperch have a unique
appearance and are identified by their
black vertical stripes. They generally have a
greenish-yellow coloration and become more
yellow during spawning. Logperch eggs stick
to the gravel substrate over which adults
prefer to spawn. They are quite voracious
and thrive on a variety of aquatic invertebrates that they acquire from turning over
small stones.

◆ **Habitat:** Larger streams and tributaries
with gravel substrate.

◆ **Range:** Widespread from the Great Lakes
to the Gulf of Mexico. In the Smokies,
Logperch are found in lower Abrams Creek,
Tabcat Creek, and the West Prong of the
Little Pigeon River.

Percina caprodes

Size: Up to 6½ in
(17 cm)

GREAT SMOKY MOUNTAINS
NATIONAL PARK

GILT DARTER

Image by Bryson Hilburn

Percina evides

Size: Up to 3½ in (9 cm)

◆ **Description:** Gilt Darters have been widely extirpated from much of their historic range but are still found in areas with good water quality and lower siltation. They can be identified by their round snout and rich orange color that males develop on their pelvic area during spawning. Females have pale white pelvic coloration. Another key characteristic is the presence of five to seven lateral blotches. Gilt Darters primarily feed on the larvae of caddisflies, mayflies, midges, and blackflies.

◆ **Habitat:** Riffle areas of clear streams with gravel or sandy substrate free of vegetation.

◆ **Range:** Fragmented range from the Great Lakes to the Mississippi River drainage. Gilt Darters are found in Little River, Abrams Creek, Oconaluftee River, and other streams draining to reservoirs of the Little Tennessee River in GSMNP.

OLIVE DARTER

Image by Jason Lins

◆ **Description:** Olive Darters are extremely rare
due to the limited availability of their preferred
habitat. Once widespread, they have become
extirpated from many areas. Populations in
the Smokies were likely once widespread
throughout tributaries of the Little Tennessee
River but are now prevented from dispersal due
to hydroelectric dams. Olive Darters can be
identified by their light olive-green coloration
and tan belly. A single black spot is found at
the base of their caudal fin. Olive Darters also
have an orange or yellow-tipped first dorsal fin
and lightly blotched lateral stripe.
◆ **Habitat:** Fast-flowing channels with boulder
or bedrock substrate.
◆ **Range:** Blue Ridge and Cumberland
Plateau regions of the Tennessee and
Cumberland rivers. In the Smokies, Olive
Darters are only found in a few tributaries of
Fontana Lake.

Percina squamata
Size: 5 in (13 cm)

GREAT SMOKY MOUNTAINS
NATIONAL PARK

WALLEYE

Image by Dave Neely

Sander vitreus
Size: Over 20 lb (9 kg)

◆ **Description:** Walleye are prized sport fish due to their large size and excellent-tasting meat. While similar in appearance to Sauger, Walleye have a few key differences. They are typically a flat green or bronze color. Walleye have a light reflecting structure in their eye, which gives them a luminous appearance and excellent night vision. Walleye also have no spots on their dorsal fin and possess a white mark on the bottom of their caudal fin. They are predators and have small, pointed teeth.

◆ **Habitat:** Cold, sandy-bottomed lakes and rivers.

◆ **Range:** Widespread throughout the Midwest, east and north to Canada. In the Smokies, Walleye are found in the embayed portion of Abrams Creek and in the Little Tennessee River system. They are also found in the Pigeon River outside the park boundary.

Image by Grant Fisher

◆ **Description:** Sauger share many similarities with Walleye but can be differentiated by the dark blotches present on their body. They also have a spotted dorsal fin that often has a notch on its lower portion. Sauger have excellent night vision and feed on smaller fish species like shad and shiners. While not as common as Walleye, Sauger can be caught using baitfish or imitations. They can live around seven years.

◆ **Habitat:** Large rivers and cold-water reservoirs. Sauger are more tolerant of turbid water than other similar fish species.

◆ **Range:** Widespread throughout the Midwest, east and north to Canada. Sauger are found in the Abrams Creek embayment as well as other embayed areas of the Little Tennessee River in the park.

Sander canadense
Size: Up to 10 lb (5 kg)

American Brook
Lamprey

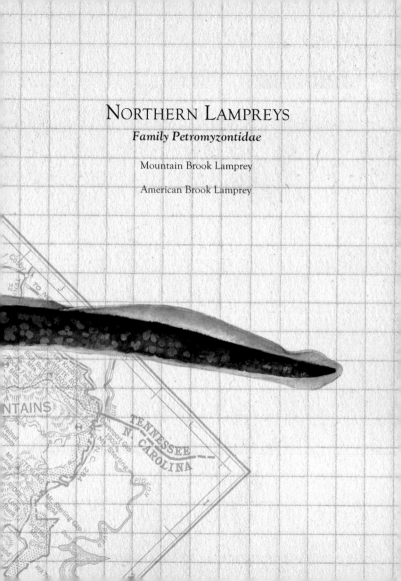

Northern Lampreys

Family Petromyzontidae

Mountain Brook Lamprey

American Brook Lamprey

MOUNTAIN BROOK LAMPREY

Image by Dave Neely

Ichthyomyzon greeleyi

Size: Up to 8 in (20 cm)

GREAT SMOKY MOUNTAINS
NATIONAL PARK

◆ **Description:** Mountain Brook Lampreys
are identified by their 53 to 62 lateral slits
called *myomeres* and olive-brown coloration.
Contrary to popular belief, not all lampreys
are parasitic. The adult Mountain Brook
Lamprey survives only on its own fat reserves.
Immature lampreys are called *ammocoetes*
and acquire food through filter feeding. The
Mountain Brook Lamprey has a cartilaginous
structure and contain no bones. This makes
it very flexible and worm-like. They live in a
blind larval form buried in sand or silt for five
to seven years before emerging as adults for a
short period of time in spring.

◆ **Habitat:** Clear streams with gravel substrate.

◆ **Range:** Upper Ohio River and Tennessee
River drainages. In the Smokies, Mountain
Brook Lampreys are found in Little River,
Oconaluftee River, Deep Creek, and
historically in Abrams Creek.

Image by Dave Neely

◆ **Description:** American Brook Lampreys can be distinguished from others by their 63 to 73 lateral slits (myomeres). They have a grayish mottled coloration. These lampreys exist in their blind filter-feeding larval form for four to six years and then emerge to spawn. During spawning, several lampreys move rocks and maintain a nest in which multiple pairs may spawn.

◆ **Habitat:** Small-to-moderate tributary streams with gravel and sand substrate.

◆ **Range:** Upper Mississippi River drainage, uplands of East Tennessee. American Brook Lampreys are found in Little River, Tabcat Creek, and historically in lower Abrams Creek in the park.

Lethenteron appendix
Size: Up to 7 in (18 cm)

GREAT SMOKY MOUNTAINS
NATIONAL PARK

Western
Mosquitofish

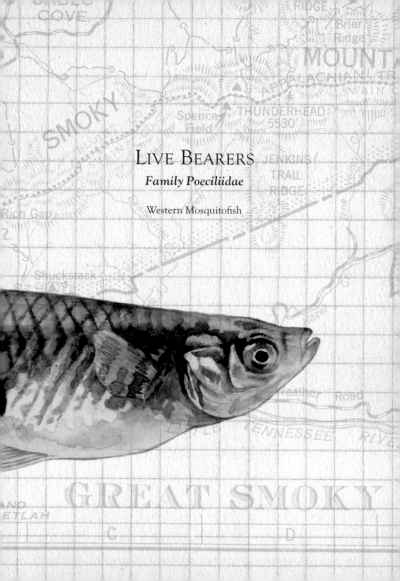

Live Bearers

Family Poeciliidae

Western Mosquitofish

WESTERN MOSQUITOFISH

Image by Nate Tessler

Gambusia affinis
Size: Up to 1 in (3 cm)

GREAT SMOKY MOUNTAINS
NATIONAL PARK

♦ **Description:** Western Mosquitofish are an introduced species. They primarily feed on mosquito larvae (Culicidae) and have been stocked in many lakes as a biological control method for mosquito populations. They are usually found near the surface and can be easily identified by their flattened head and upturned mouth. In the same family as Guppies (the popular aquarium fish), Western Mosquitofish are livebearers. The female gives birth to her young and does not lay eggs. They are an extremely hardy fish and have been used for toxicity studies by many institutions.

♦ **Habitat:** Shallow backwater of lakes, swamps, and streams.

♦ **Range:** Found throughout the Mobile River drainage west to California. In the Smokies, Western Mosquitofish are found in Tabcat Creek as well as other embayed areas of the Little Tennessee River.

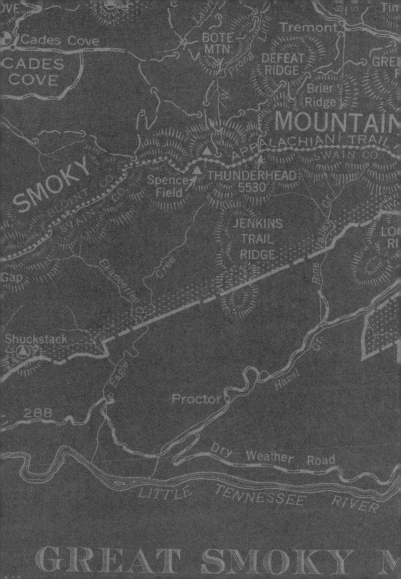

Northern Studfish

Topminnows

Family Fundulidae

Northern Studfish

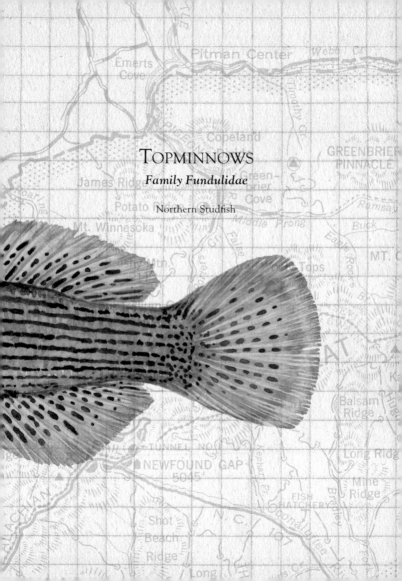

NORTHERN STUDFISH

Image by Bryson Hilburn

Fundulus catenatus
Size: Up to 7 in (18 cm)

GREAT SMOKY MOUNTAINS
NATIONAL PARK

◆ **Description:** Northern Studfish are in the topminnow family and, as such, primarily dwell near the surface. They can be distinguished by their upward-facing, superior mouth. During spawning, males develop an electric blue color with bright orange dotted lines. Northern Studfish have a diet composed of aquatic insects and small snails. They can live up to five years.

◆ **Habitat:** Often found in vegetated areas or gravel beds of moderate-sized streams.

◆ **Range:** Tennessee and Cumberland river drainages. Also found in other areas of the Mississippi River drainage. In the Smokies, Northern Studfish were historically found in Abrams Creek, but they can still be found in the Little River at the park boundary.

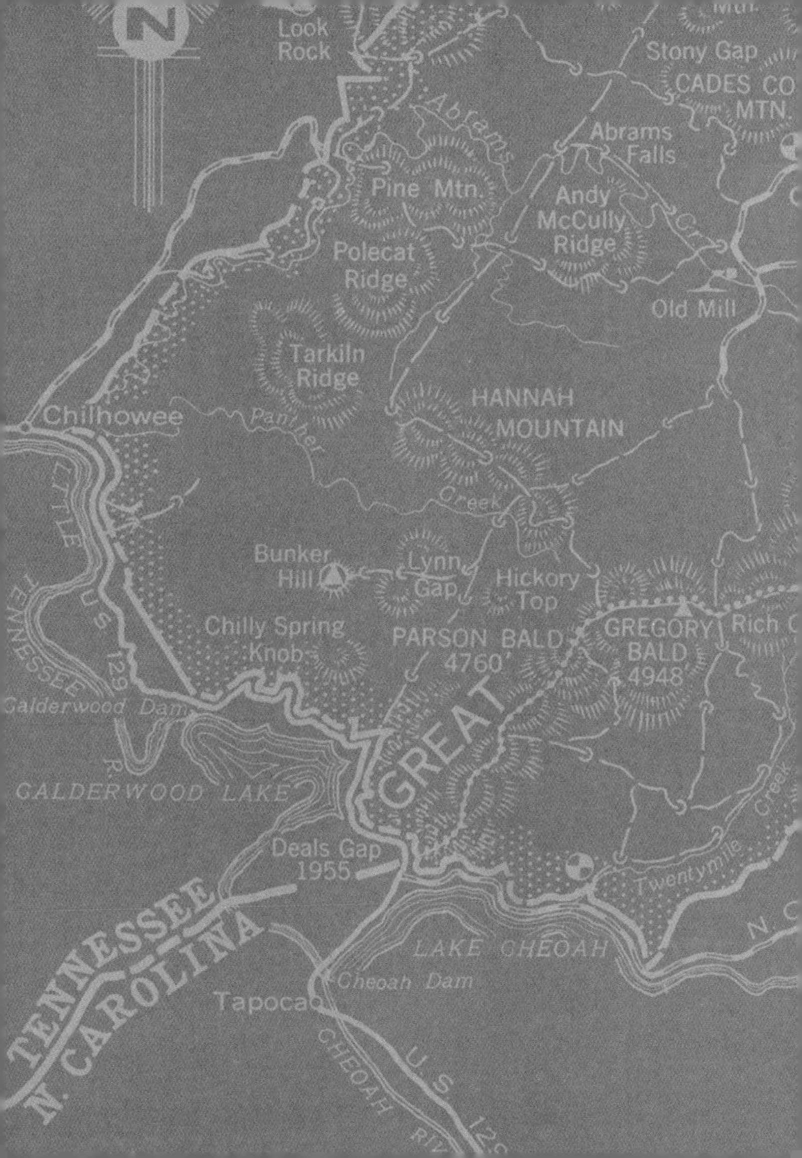

N
Look Rock
Stony Gap
CADES CO
MTN.
Abrams
Abrams Falls
Pine Mtn.
Andy McCully Ridge
Polecat Ridge
Old Mill
Tarkiln Ridge
HANNAH MOUNTAIN
Chilhowee
Panther
Creek
LITTLE
TENNESSEE
US
129
Bunker Hill
Lynn Gap
Hickory Top
Chilly Spring Knob
PARSON BALD 4760'
GREGORY BALD 4948
Rich
Calderwood Dam
R.
GALDERWOOD LAKE
GREAT
Deals Gap 1955
Twentymile
Creek
TENNESSEE
N. CAROLINA
LAKE CHEOAH
Cheoah Dam
Tapoca
CHEOAH RIV
US
129

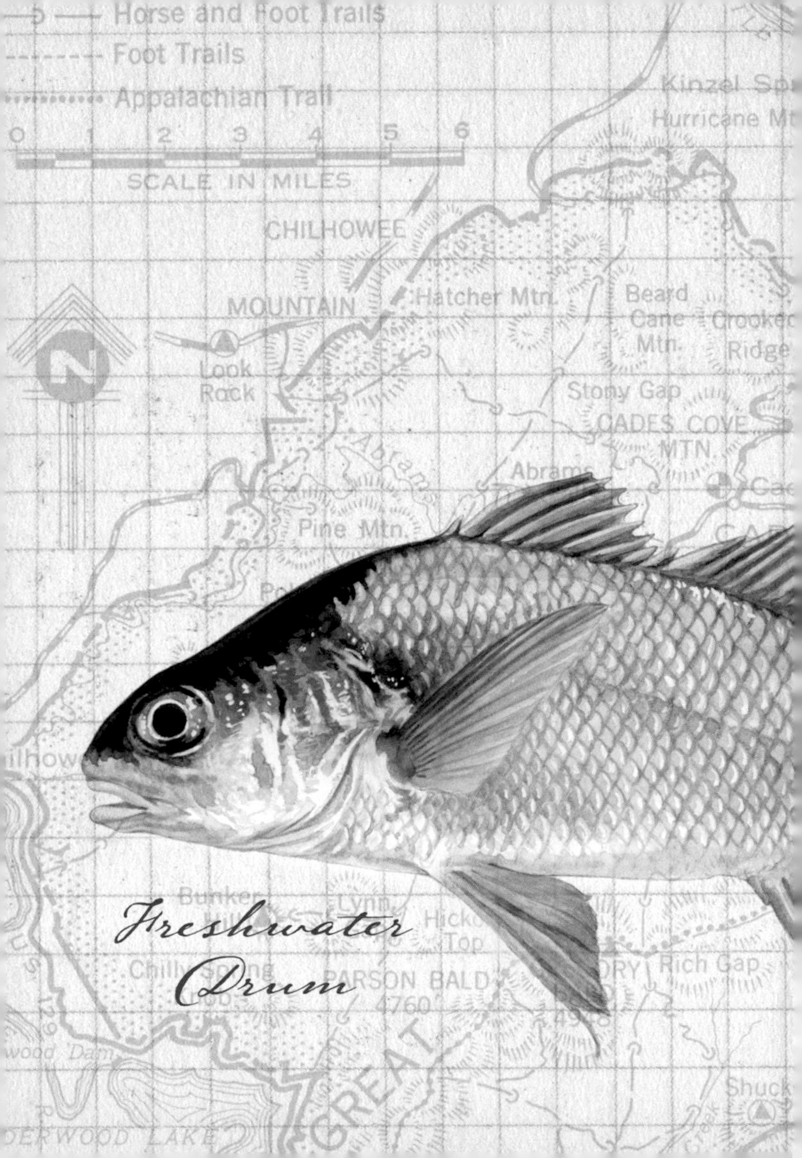

Kinzel Sp
Hurricane Mt

CHILHOWEE

N

MOUNTAIN   Hatcher Mtn.   Beard
Cane Crooked
Mtn.   Ridge

Look
Rock

Stony Gap

CADES COVE
MTN.

Abrams   Abrams

Pine Mtn.

Cae

CA

ilhow

Freshwater
Drum

Bunker   Lynn
Hick
Top

Chilly   PARSON BALD   DRY Rich Gap
4760

wood Dam

129

Shuck

GREAT

DERWOOD LAKE

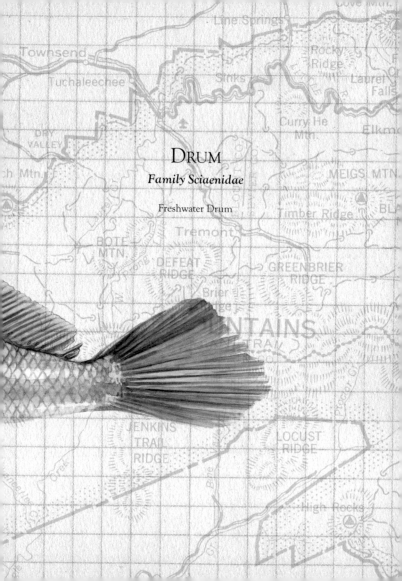

Drum

Family Sciaenidae

Freshwater Drum

FRESHWATER DRUM

Image by Dave Neely

Aplodinotus grunniens

Size: Most under 10 lb (5 kg)

GREAT SMOKY MOUNTAINS NATIONAL PARK

◆ **Description:** Freshwater Drum are named for the unique thumping noise that the fish make using their air bladder. They are easily identifiable by their grayish-gold color and large, humped back. Anglers acquire "lucky stones" by removing the drum's otoliths. These are rounded bony structures that fish use to gain a sense of balance while swimming. Freshwater Drum have a diverse diet that includes aquatic insects, crustaceans, and smaller fish as well as mollusks. Most Freshwater Drum are under 10 pounds, but they can grow to over 50 pounds. Many anglers catch them while bottom fishing with cut bait or with minnow imitation lures.

◆ **Habitat:** Large rivers and lakes.

◆ **Range:** Mississippi River and Great Lakes drainages. In the Smokies, Freshwater Drum are found within reservoir areas of the Little Tennessee River and can swim into lower portions of its tributary streams.

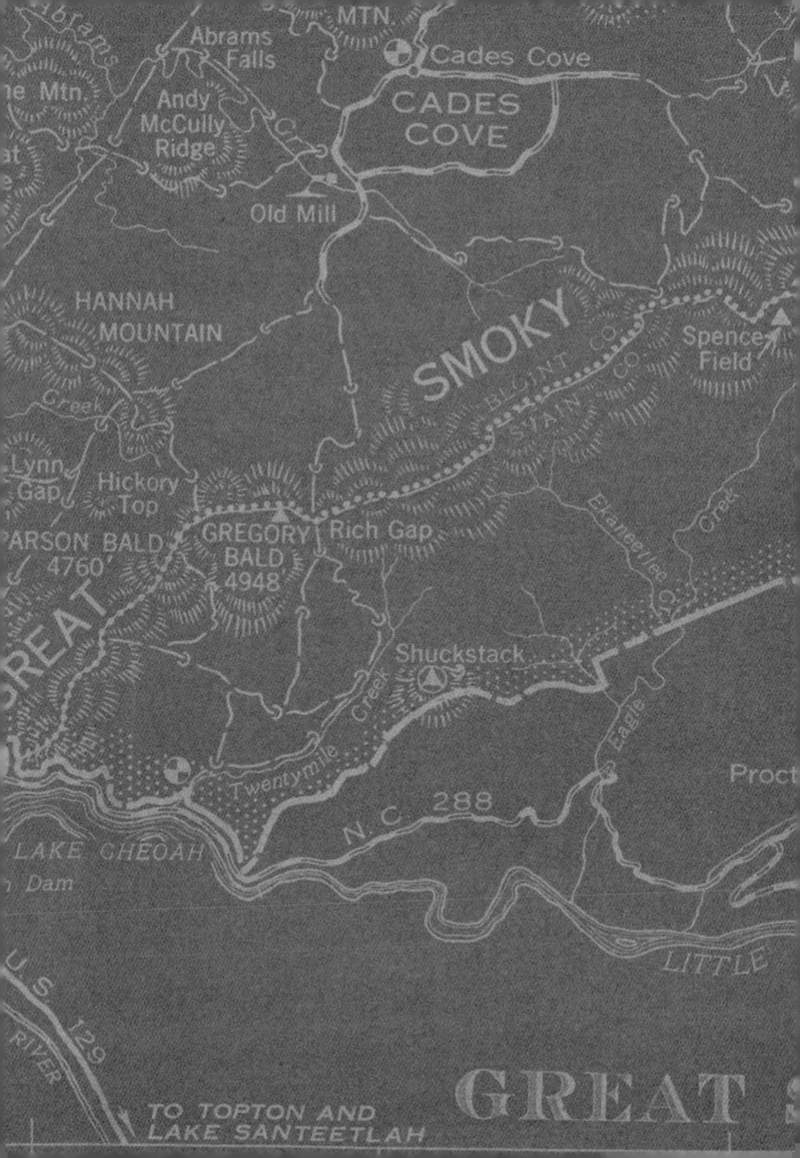

MTN.
Abrams Falls
Cades Cove
CADES COVE
Andy McCully Ridge
Old Mill
HANNAH MOUNTAIN
Creek
SMOKY
BLOUNT CO.
SWAIN CO.
Spence Field
Lynn Gap
Hickory Top
GREGORY BALD 4948'
Rich Gap
PARSON BALD 4760'
GREAT
Ekaneetlee Cr.
Creek
Shuckstack
Twentymile Creek
Eagle
Proct
N.C. 288
LAKE CHEOAH
Dam
LITTLE
U.S. 129
RIVER
TO TOPTON AND LAKE SANTEETLAH
GREAT

Rainbow Trout

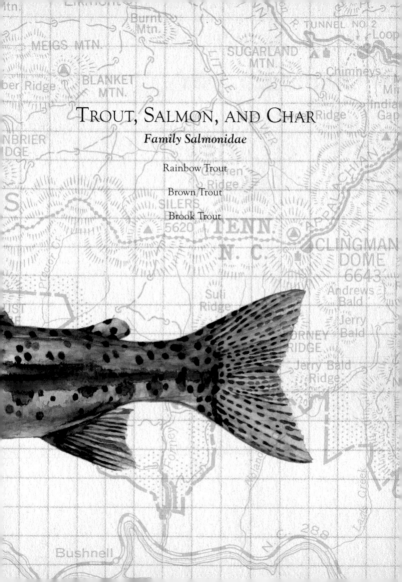

TROUT, SALMON, AND CHAR

Family Salmonidae

Rainbow Trout

Brown Trout

Brook Trout

RAINBOW TROUT

Image by Grant Fisher

Oncorhynchus mykiss

Size: Up to 12 in (30 cm)

GREAT SMOKY MOUNTAINS
NATIONAL PARK

◆ **Description:** Of the three trout species found in the Smokies, Rainbow Trout are by far the most common. While not native, they were stocked in the early 1900s to replace Brook Trout populations that had been lost due to logging operations. Their body is covered in small black spots. Laterally, Rainbow Trout have a pinkish-red stripe with purple blotches that fade as the fish ages. They are very aggressive feeders and quickly outcompete other trout species. Rainbow Trout are predators and feed on smaller fish, aquatic invertebrates, and even salamanders. While wild trout over 12 inches are rare, stockers can grow over three feet. Anglers catch Rainbow Trout on a variety of lures from flies to spinners.

◆ **Habitat:** Wide range of habitats in streams and lakes.

◆ **Range:** Native to western United States but have been stocked extensively elsewhere. Rainbow Trout can be found in all Smokies stream systems up to 4,000 feet.

BROWN TROUT

Image by Adam Walker

♦ **Description:** Brown Trout are the largest and most warmwater tolerant trout found in the Smokies. They can grow to over three feet and weigh up to 40 pounds. Brown Trout in the two-foot range are not uncommon in larger park streams, which makes them prized by anglers. They are recognizable by their brown-tan body color and are covered in black dorsal spots and red lateral spots. Brown Trout

Salmo trutta

Size: Up to 3 ft
(91 cm)

GREAT SMOKY MOUNTAINS
NATIONAL PARK

are more piscivorous than other trout and feed almost exclusively on minnows, darters, sculpin, and even smaller trout. Larger male specimens can develop a "kype," which is a hooked lower jaw similar to salmon. Occasionally, male Brook Trout fertilize Brown Trout eggs, creating the hybrid Tiger Trout.

♦ **Habitat:** Wide range of habitats in streams and lake tailwaters.

♦ **Range:** Native to Europe but widely introduced in the United States. In the Smokies, Brown Trout can be found in the Little, Oconaluftee, Little Tennessee, and Pigeon river systems.

BROOK TROUT

Image by Grant Fisher

Salvelinus fontinalis

Size: Up to 6 in (15 cm)

GREAT SMOKY MOUNTAINS
NATIONAL PARK

◆ **Description:** As the only native trout species to the region, Brook Trout are hidden gems in the Smokies. Runoff from logging operations in the early 1900s decimated their populations. Efforts are actively underway to restore Brook Trout back to much of their historic range in the park. They can be identified by their olive-brown coloration, bright orange belly, and red lateral spots. Brook Trout are the smallest species of trout in the Smokies and are surprisingly short lived. Few live longer than three years, and some never exceed six inches. Due to the extreme conditions they live in, Brook Trout over ten inches are rare. They feed on aquatic invertebrates and small fish when present. Many anglers enjoy the challenge of fishing for this elusive fish using flies, small spinners, or soft plastic lures.

◆ **Habitat:** Small, clear, high-elevation streams up to 5,000 feet.

◆ **Range:** Canada and Hudson Bay, south to Southern Appalachians. Brook Trout are found in high-elevation streams draining into the Pigeon, Little Pigeon, Oconaluftee, Little Tennessee, and Little rivers.

MOUNTAINS

Rocky Face
Mtn.

Camel
Hump
Mtn.

Chestnut Br.

Mt. Sterling

N.C.

284

PIGEON

Big

Cr.

Walnut
Bottom

Gunter Fk.

OT 6621'

STERLING

Mt.
Sterling

RIDGE

Mt. Sterling Gap
3894

Dam

River

BALSAM
MTN.

CO

wano
dge

Pretty
Hollow Gap

Big
Cataloochee
Knob

Long
Bunk

Indian
Ridge

Short
Bunk

Scottish
Mtn.

Creek

WATERV
LAK

BUTT
MOUNTAIN

Noland
Mtn.

Beech
Ridge

Canadian
Top

Co
Creek
40

Pin Oak
Gap

Cataloochee

Shanty
Mountain

Wash
Ridge

Cataloochee

Den
Ridge

Cove
Cree

Spruce Mtn.
Ridge

Big
Fork
Ridge

Caldwell Fk.

CATALOO-
CHEE

Fk.

Chil-
oskie
idge

BALSAM

MTN.

Rough

Fk.

Caldwell

Horse
Pen
Ridge

DIVIDE

Big
Ridge

McClure
Ridge

Heintooga
Overlook

Maggot
Ridge

Double Gap

Overlook
Ridge

Pauls Gap

Pine Tree Gap

Little Bald Knob
Sheepback

GLOSSARY

ADIPOSE FIN Small fleshy fin located between the dorsal (top) and caudal (tail) fin. The function of adipose fins is not fully understood, but they do aid fish somewhat in stabilization. Adipose fins are frequently clipped to mark fishes for study.

ANAL FIN Fin located on the ventral (bottom) side of a fish between the pelvic fins and caudal fin. Anal fins provide additional stability while swimming.

BARBELS Whisker-like structures found on catfish and carp. Barbels function as sensory organs to detect food sources in dark or murky water.

BENTHIC Being associated with the bottom of a stream, lake, or pond.

CAUDAL FIN The tail fin of a fish. The caudal fin is the primary structure responsible for propelling fish through water.

DORSAL The top view of a fish along its back.

DORSAL FIN The main fin on a fish's backside. The dorsal fin primarily serves to prevent fish from rolling during a turn while swimming. Some fish such as darters and sculpin have two dorsal fins.

EMBAYMENT Portion of a stream that flows into a reservoir. Embayed portions of a stream lose the natural riffle, run, and pool characteristics and resemble a lake.

KERATINOUS Being made of keratin. Keratin is a type of fibrous protein that makes up hair, nails, horns, and claws in many animals.

LATERAL LINE Line in fish scales that is made up of sensory organs. Fish use these to detect movement and vibrations.

MACROINVERTEBRATES Animals lacking a backbone but large enough to see without using a microscope.

MYOMERES Sections of skeletal muscle tissue that appear as lines of muscle fibers. They are used to bend and flex the body.

OMNIVORE Organism that feeds on both plants and animals.

OPERCULUM Bony structures that support a fish's face and provide a protective covering to the gills.

OTOLITHS Boney disks near the brain that function as a fish's middle ear and help them maintain equilibrium.

PECTORAL FIN Used to make quick, abrupt movements when swimming. Pectoral fins assist certain fish with vertical movement and stabilization when resting on the streambed.

PELVIC FIN Located between the pectoral and anal fins. Pelvic fins help fish maintain an upright position when swimming.

PISCIVORE Organism that primarily feeds on fishes.

PLANKTIVORE Organism that feeds on zooplankton and phytoplankton.

POOL Slow moving, typically deeper area of a stream.

RESERVOIR Artificial lake usually created by construction of a hydroelectric dam that functions for recreation as well a water and power source.

RIFFLE Shallow, rocky section of stream with swift current.

RUN Area of moderate current typically occurring after a riffle.

SUBTERMINAL Downward facing. Fishes with subterminal mouths are typically adapted to feed on the stream bottom.

SUPERIOR Upward facing.

Fishes with superior mouths are topwater feeders.

SWIM BLADDER Internal organ that fishes use to move up and down in the water. Fishes can fill the bladder with air to increase buoyancy and deflate to dive. This allows them to maintain their location in the water column. Not all fishes possess a swim bladder.

TERMINAL Forward facing. Fishes that have a terminal mouth feed in the mid-level of a stream.

TOOTH PATCH Rough or pointed structure on a fish's tongue that aids in holding food items while feeding and swallowing.

TRIBUTARY Stream that flows into a larger river or lake.

TUBERCLES Small rounded keratinous nodules that form on male fishes during spawning season. They function as a secondary sex characteristic.

VENTRAL The bottom view of a fish from its underbelly.

WEIR Structure built to capture large groups of migrating fish for harvest. Weirs are typically constructed in a V shape. Fishes enter the large end and become trapped at the small end.

SPECIES INDEX
Common and scientific names

WORKS CONSULTED AND FURTHER READING

Etnier, David A., and Wayne C. Starnes. *The Fishes of Tennessee.* Knoxville: University of Tennessee Press, 2001.

Page, Lawrence M., and Brooks M. Burr. *Peterson Field Guide to Freshwater Fishes.* 2nd ed. Boston: Houghton Mifflin Harcourt, 2011.

North American Native Fishes Association, nanfa.org.

Tennessee Aquarium Freshwater Information Network, tnacifin.com.

United States Geological Survey, usgs.org.

About the Author

Grant Fisher is a native of Sevier County, Tennessee, where he enjoys exploring the mountains he calls home. He earned a bachelor's degree in environmental studies from Carson-Newman University and a master's degree from the Department of Forestry, Wildlife, and Fisheries at the University of Tennessee in Knoxville. His master's work focused on determining the effect of stream restoration designs in urban environments on functional lift of aquatic insect and fish communities. Grant has also worked as an employee for the National Park Service in Great Smoky Mountains National Park. There he conducted park-wide vital signs surveys of fish and aquatic insect species, helped restore populations of native Brook Trout, systemically treated eastern hemlock trees against the infamous hemlock woolly adelgid, and removed exotic plant species from sensitive habitat areas.